K·I·S·S

DK

The Only Guides You'll Ever Need!

THIS SERIES IS YOUR TRUSTED GUIDE through all of life's stages and situations. Want to learn how to surf the Internet or care for your new dog? Or maybe you'd like to become a wine connoisseur or an expert gardener? The solution is simple: just pick up a K.I.S.S. Guide and turn to the first page.

Expert authors will walk you through the subject from start to finish, using simple blocks of knowledge to build your skills one step at a time. Build upon these learning blocks and by the end of the book, you'll be an expert yourself! Or, if you are familiar with the topic but want to learn more, it's easy to dive in and pick up where you left off.

The K.I.S.S. Guides deliver what they promise: simple access to all the information you'll need on one subject. Other titles you might want to check out include: Playing Guit... Cat Care, Living With a Dog, Astrology, Sex, Weight Loss, an...

GUIDE TO

Photography

JOHN GARRETT

Foreword by **Martin Sandler**
Acclaimed Author and Photohistorian

A Dorling Kindersley Book

LONDON, NEW YORK,
MUNICH, MELBOURNE, DELHI

Dorling Kindersley Limited
Managing Editor Maxine Lewis
Managing Art Editor Heather McCarry

Production Heather Hughes
Category Publisher Mary Thompson

Produced for Dorling Kindersley by **Sands Publishing Solutions**
4 Jenner Way, Eccles, Aylesford, Kent ME20 7SQ

Project Editors David & Sylvia Tombesi-Walton
Project Art Editor Simon Murrell

First published in 2001 by Dorling Kindersley Limited
80 Strand, London WC2R 0RL

A Penguin Company

2 4 6 8 10 9 7 5 3 1

A CIP catalogue record for this book is available
from the British Library.

ISBN 1 4053 0181 3

Colour reproduction by ColourScan, Singapore
Printed and bound by Printer Portuguesa, Portugal

For our complete catalogue visit

www.dk.com

Contents at a Glance

PART ONE

Before You Shoot

PART TWO

The Point-and-Shoot

PART THREE

The Arty Stuff

PART FOUR

Photographic Themes

PART FIVE

Taking Things More Seriously

CONTENTS

PART ONE Before You Shoot

CHAPTER 1   The History of Photography   22

CHAPTER 2   How the Camera Works   34

PART THREE The Arty Stuff

PART FOUR Photographic Themes

PART FIVE Taking Things More Seriously

Foreword

"I HAVE SEIZED THE LIGHT." With that proud exclamation, in 1839, Louis Jacques Mandé Daguerre announced that he had succeeded in producing the world's first successful photograph. Less than 50 years later, George Eastman would invent the Kodak® camera, making just about everyone a photographer and a picture-maker. Within a remarkably short period of time thereafter, photography would become such an important part of our lives that critic Thomas Lawson could proclaim in truth that "photography is the modern world".

Put simply, photography has become the most democratic form of art the world has ever known. It has established itself as the universal language, understood by everyone, arguably surpassing even the written word as a form of communication.

Almost all of us take pictures. We use our photographs as memories – memories of the rituals and passages in our lives, reminders of ourselves and our loved ones in earlier times, records of places we have lived or visited. And photography provides us personally with even more. In our hands, the camera gives us nothing less than one of our most powerful means of self-expression.

Yes, most of us are picture-takers. And almost all of us wish we were better at it. Now, thanks to John Garrett and what he has given us in this book, we can be. Here I would add a word of caution. Don't be misled by how easy this book is to read or how enjoyable it is to look at its compelling photographs.

This is the most solid and helpful book of its type I have encountered. It will not only make you a better photographer, it will help you understand what it is about certain photographs that makes them so highly regarded.

Garrett touches all the bases. He explains the many technical aspects of picture-taking in easy-to-understand, practical terms. He identifies the special challenges of taking specific types of pictures – portraits, landscapes, still lifes, snapshots, action, and travel photographs – and provides us with achievable strategies and tips for most effectively capturing each type of image. Throughout the book he offers particularly valuable advice on how to master what successful photographers have long known to be the three most basic elements that lead to great photographs – light, composition, and capturing the decisive moment.

It was that giant of the medium Edward Weston who reminded us that photography is the most pure and direct means of expression yet discovered, and that the person behind the camera is limited only by his or her capacity to create. This book will help you increase that capacity. And along with taking better pictures, you will receive an invaluable bonus. Through the content and approach of this book, John Garrett has helped us better understand one of the greatest gifts that photography has to offer – its ability to expand our vision and see the world in a whole new way.

MARTIN SANDLER

Introduction

WELCOME TO the K.I.S.S. Guide to Photography. I have written this book with the intention of simplifying the seemingly complicated and technical process of photography – to demystify the whole thing.

I've been a professional photographer for nearly 40 years but I don't believe in technique for the sake of it. Neither do I drool at the sight of a new camera. I am interested in producing good images, and strive constantly to improve my photography so that I can achieve personal satisfaction by taking a beautiful picture that was previously beyond my expertise.

The photographic principles discussed in this book apply equally to the point-and-shoot photographers as they do to the SLR users, and although there are some chapters that seem, on the surface, to be devoted specifically to one or the other, I believe you will benefit from reading everything in the book.

I hope that this guide will provide the perfect starting point for all the newcomers among you and kick-start in you a thirst for photographic knowledge wherever you can find it. To help you out with that, I've included a recommended-reading list and a whole bunch of web sites in the appendices. But don't stop there; check out your local camera clubs and night classes, too.

Even if you're not a newcomer there's still plenty here for you. I think you'll find the sections on light and composition to be creatively stimulating, for example, and I am passing on tips for all the great themes of photography. These are nuggets of knowledge and advice that have come from hard-earned experience... not to mention costly mistakes.

On the subject of mistakes.... In writing this book I tried to bear in mind several goals, one of which was to help you reduce your number of goof-ups. But even so, don't be too discouraged when you get something wrong. We've all been there.

To me, one of the joys of photography is that we are all lifelong students: I aspire to be a better photographer next month than I am now.

In this early part of the 21st century, digital photography is very much with us and I've included two chapters on that subject. However, if you are into this sort of photography, you should note that the shooting method is similar enough to conventional photography for the whole book to be applicable to you too.

So there's something for everyone here. Regardless of what sort of camera you are using or your level of expertise, if you are interested in photography and improving your photographic skills, you've come to the right place.

Have fun, folks – that's the whole point!

JOHN GARRETT

A NOTE ON MEASUREMENT CONVENTIONS IN PHOTOGRAPHY

Measurements are used for many different reasons in photography, and photographic convention decrees that some measurements are always given in metric and some in imperial. In the great majority of cases in this book I have not converted one into the other: if something is always given one way, it serves no purpose to learn it another way. However, where I have felt that confusion may be caused by *not* giving a conversion – when talking about medium format cameras, for example – I have included one, at least in the first occasion of its use.

What's Inside?

THE INFORMATION in the K.I.S.S. Guide to Photography is arranged from the simple to the more advanced, making it most effective if you start from the beginning and slowly work your way through to the more involved chapters.

PART ONE

I thought it would be a good idea to give you some background information on photography before we get into the nitty-gritty of how to take pictures. In Part One, I'll tell you a little about the history of photography and then move on to how cameras work and the wide choice in the shops today, as well as the complicated issue of film types.

PART TWO

Compact cameras are serious machines, far more sophisticated than the cameras used to shoot many of our favourite images from the past. But they can't take beautiful pictures by themselves. In this part we'll look at the different types of point-and-shoot available and how to control all that automation to make the camera do what you want it to.

PART THREE

I've called Part Three The Arty Stuff, and I mean it in a good way. Arty is inspirational and is at the core of the best of us, both as people and as communities. I believe that you will produce more interesting pictures than you do now if you get into the arty stuff, and you'll get a lot more satisfaction from your work.

PART FOUR

In Part Four, I have grouped classic photography subjects into themes. This section is mostly about how you learn to see the world as a photographer. It's about becoming more visually aware, and it's also about simplifying photography. I want you to be able to take great pictures... and to learn from my experience.

PART FIVE

This last section of the book is intended to inspire you to go on further than you first thought you would. We'll look at the equipment professional photographers use, black-and-white photography, what happens after your roll of film is all finished – the important behind-the-scenes bit – and I'll shed some light on digital photography.

The Extras

THROUGHOUT THE BOOK you will notice a number of boxes and symbols. They are there to emphasize certain points I want you to pay special attention to, because they are important to your understanding and improvement. You'll find:

Very Important Point

This symbol points out a topic I believe deserves careful attention. You really need to know this information before continuing.

Complete No-No

This is a warning, something I want to advise you not to do or to be aware of.

Getting Technical

When the information is about to get a bit technical, I'll let you know so that you can read carefully.

Inside Scoop

These are special suggestions that come from my own personal experience. I want to share them with you because they helped me when I was learning the game.

You'll also find some little boxes that include information I think is important, useful, or just plain fun.

Trivia...
These are simply fun facts or anecdotes that will give you an extra appreciation and understanding of photography.

DEFINITION
Here I'll define words and terms for you in an easy-to-understand style. You'll also find a glossary at the back of the book packed with photography lingo.

INTERNET
www.dk.com

I think the Internet is a great resource for photographers, so I've scouted out some web sites that I think will add to your enjoyment and understanding of the subject.

PART ONE

WE'RE GOING ON A PHOTOGRAPHIC JOURNEY...

BEFORE YOU SHOOT

I THOUGHT IT WOULD BE a good idea to give you some background information on photography before we get into the nitty-gritty of taking pictures. Some of you will already know more than others, but it's important to learn a little about the *history* of photography before we move on to the camera itself.

The advances that have been made in photography since the first pictures in the mid-19th century are *mind-blowing*. However, it's nice to feel connected to those old pioneers who had to work so hard to pave the way for the simplicity we have today. This part is also about how cameras work and the options we have when we choose what to buy next, as well as the complicated issue of *film types*. This is all stuff that you need to know in order to get the most out of photography.

Chapter 1

The History of Photography

THE FIRST THING I WANT TO DO in this book is run through a potted history of photography so far. It will hopefully give you an understanding of some of the extraordinary progress that has been made in such a short time. I feel almost overawed when I study some of the fantastic photographs that have been taken in the past, often with very rudimentary equipment. When I read about 19th-century photographers it spurs me on to make even more of an effort to improve my own work. I hope this chapter will inspire you in the same way.

In this chapter...

✓ The birth of photography

✓ The photography explosion

✓ Photography for the masses

✓ Keeping things simple

✓ The modern compact

The birth of photography

PHOTOGRAPHY WAS OFFICIALLY INVENTED in 1839. I say "officially" because that is when the existence of a photographic image was made public. Amazingly, though, the first reference to cameras is recorded by Aristotle in the 4th century BC.

The *camera obscura* was originally a completely enclosed, dark room with a hole in one wall, which, by the effect of light diffraction, projected an image of the outside world on to the opposite wall. It was not until 1568, around 2,000 years later, that Italian Daniello Barbaro added a lens to the hole, greatly improving the sharpness of the image. In the mid-17th century the camera obscura became portable when it was miniaturized down to a box about 30 cm (12 inches) square. When a piece of paper was placed opposite the lens it was possible to display landscape pictures on it. Everything was in place for photography, except the chemistry.

PORTABLE CAMERA OBSCURA

> **DEFINITION**
>
> Camera obscura is a Latin term literally meaning "dark room", or "dark chamber".

The first pictures

It was known in the late 18th century that an image (from a stencil) could be formed on material soaked in silver nitrate, but there was no means of fixing that image until Sir John Herschel discovered sodium hyposulphite as a fixing agent in 1819... and we were all set.

By 1819 we had a camera, photographic-sensitive materials, and a fixing agent, and in the summer of 1826 a Frenchman named Joseph Niepce made the first photograph. He cut a hole in a wooden box and into the hole he fitted a lens. Opposite the lens he placed a glass plate coated with a bitumen compound. He placed the box on his workshop's windowsill and left it for 8 hours.

When he finally removed the box from the windowsill he washed the plate in lavender oil. Where the plate had been exposed to the light, the bitumen had hardened. The unexposed areas of the plate dissolved in the oil, leaving behind a crude photographic image of the rooftops in his village.

In 1829, Niepce went into collaboration with another Frenchman called Louis Daguerre. Together, through further experimentation, they developed the daguerreotype method of photography, which was announced to the world by the Institut de France in 1839. Daguerre excitedly said, "I have seized the fleeting light and imprisoned it.... I have forced the sun to paint pictures for me."

Fox Talbot

At the same time as Niepce and Daguerre were developing the daguerreotype, Englishman William Fox Talbot was working on his own experiments in photographic imaging. Each party was totally unaware of the work being carried out by the other. Fox Talbot was horrified by the Institut de France's announcement in 1839. He thought he had invented photography. He had certainly succeeded in making photographic images, but unfortunately they weren't permanent.

In 1841 Fox Talbot developed the first negative-to-positive process, a process that was repeatable, meaning that black-and-white prints were now possible.

He soaked high-grade writing paper in a salt solution, and, after it had dried, he brushed the paper with a silver-nitrate solution, forming a light-sensitive silver chloride. Once that had dried, he placed the paper in his camera and removed the lens cap to expose it. He was left with a negative image that he was able to stabilize with a strong salt solution. To make a positive print of that image, he put the negative in contact with another sheet and exposed it to light again. This was an incredible step forward – a leap is probably more accurate – because it was now possible to reproduce prints from a negative at will and in as many numbers as required. Now photography took off... big time! I'll leave it to the historians to decide who invented photography, but I believe that Fox Talbot was the father of modern photography.

WILLIAM FOX TALBOT

INTERNET

www.rleggat.com/
photohistory

If you want a bit more information about some of photography's pioneers, this is a great place to start. Not only has Dr Robert Leggat put together a history of the art form up until the 1920s, but he's also cross-referenced all the key names: just click on a name in the text to jump to the relevant biography.

The photography explosion

THE VICTORIANS BECAME OBSESSED with photography, and by 1853 there were 80 professional studios in New York alone. London and Paris were also photo mad.

Frederick Scott Archer made a big contribution to the photography explosion by giving us the collodion plate, which basically enabled the making of negatives on glass plates. Unfortunately, though, the process worked best when the silver nitrate was wet. This meant photographers had to travel with a light-tight tent darkroom, a camera, a tripod, water, and a heavy load of glass plates and liquid silver solution.

They set up the camera, went into the tent and coated the glass plate, exposed it in the camera, and then went back into the darkroom to develop the plate. Just give a thought to those guys when you next take your APS camera out of your pocket and snap away!

> **DEFINITION**
>
> APS stands for Advanced Photo System, which was launched in the mid-1990s.

You can still buy bottles of liquid photographic emulsion and coat your own glass plates, but this method is mainly used by arty printmakers who are looking for unusual effects.

Recording the world

Those wet-plate photographers travelled all over the world and documented the Civil War and the Crimean War carrying equipment weighing hundreds of pounds on their backs. They were heroic in their devotion to recording the world around them. For the first time in history the public could see what celebrities looked like. The great migration west in America was now being photographed, as were the great industrial and architectural projects. Photojournalism was alive and kicking, and the world was about to become smaller.

■ *Images such as this gave the general public a chance to see sights that they had only ever read or heard about before.*

Photography for the masses

IN THE EARLY 1880s, *the revolutionary gelatine dry plate was invented and put on the market. This was important because it meant that photographers no longer had to lug around a portable darkroom and all the other stuff I've talked about in the last couple of pages.*

The dry plates were much more sensitive to light, so instantaneous pictures were now possible. Instead of covering and uncovering the lens to make an exposure, the *shutter* was added to the camera. It was this advancement that changed the look of photography dramatically. You could now photograph movement: no longer would a horse and cart walking down the road be blurred. People didn't suddenly become happier in the 1880s, but they were finally allowed to smile when photographed and were no longer required to sit with their heads clamped to keep them still for a 15- to 30-second exposure. Exposures (depending on the light quality) were now around ⅕ of a second. On a sunny day, it was even possible to take hand-held pictures.

> **DEFINITION**
>
> *The **shutter** is the mechanism used to control when and for how long the film inside the camera is exposed to light. It is activated by pressing the button that "takes the picture". The button is correctly called the shutter button or shutter-release button.*

Don't throw away your grandfather's old camera. Those machines are now very collectable.

■ **Family portraits** *were hugely popular in the early years of photography – just as they were in paintings before photography existed – and still are today.*

Kodak gets us at it!

In 1885 an American named George Eastman made another very important invention. He coated a light-sensitive silver solution onto rolls of paper to make the first photographic film.

Three years later, in 1888, Eastman created the famous Kodak® trademark and was totally responsible for popularizing photography by launching a camera already loaded with film, with the potential for 100 snaps. The camera had a fixed focus and fixed shutter speed. There was nothing to do but point and shoot. The famous Kodak slogan "You press the button, we do the rest" kicked off photography as a pastime for the masses.

> **DEFINITION**
>
> *The trademark **Kodak** is a word George Eastman made up – he just liked the sound of it. He also thought the visual appearance of it would look good and be remembered. It doesn't mean anything!*

Once the photographer had finished all of the film, he returned the camera to Kodak. The company processed and printed the pictures, reloaded the camera with a new film, and returned the whole lot to the photographer. These days, well over 100 years later, we still buy single-use cameras – is nothing new?

Trivia...

My first camera was a Kodak Box Brownie. I thought it took great pictures. In fact, the quality was far inferior to the single-use compact cameras that are so cheap today.

■ **George Eastman**, *the man behind the Kodak company, was responsible for making photography affordable for the population at large.*

Slow times

The next 30 years or so did not see any major revolutions in photography. Great developments were made, but in stages rather than in leaps and bounds. Amateurs were snapping away with their box cameras and bellows roll-film cameras while the professionals stuck to their serious, large format machines. Although there was some wonderful reportage work being done in that period by the likes of Alfred Stieglitz, the main thrust was to try to establish photography as a major art form. As a result this was a rich period for images: check out the work of Edward Steichen, Paul Strand, and some of the other Pictorialist photographers.

The movies were where the biggest breakthroughs were being made, and it was the great success of 35mm film in cinema photography that gave birth to the 35mm rangefinder camera.

EARLY KODAK CAMERA

Enter Leica

The first 35mm stills camera was launched in 1925, when the German company Leica introduced the Leica 1, developed by Oskar Barnack. This camera revolutionized the hand-held camera market. It was the first serious "miniature" camera (a term coined by the trade at the time) that enabled photographers to capture reality spontaneously and to observe life as it was going on around them.

The Leica 1 was a fraction of the size and weight of the large format press cameras, which used glass plates and sheet film. It had a high-definition lens and a rudimentary manual-focusing system. The aperture and shutter speed were also manual and, since there were no light meters on the market at that time, exposure times had to be judged from experience.

These early 35mm cameras were the great-grandparents of our modern compacts, and for us happy snappers of the 21st century, the *point-and-shoot* was in the pipeline from the day the idea for the Leica 1 was born.

DEFINITION

Point-and-shoot *is the name often given to compact cameras, simply because it more or less defines the actions needed to take a photograph with those machines. The trade and professional photographers tend to use the term compact camera instead.*

Photojournalism

The photographers using these new lightweight machines started to show people images that previously they had had to conjure up in their own mind's eye from the written word. Photojournalism had arrived.

■ **Photojournalists** *recorded not only the major news stories of the day, but also documented more everyday subjects like sporting events. People all around the world were even able to see what their contemporaries in other countries wore to watch their national sports.*

The invention of the first 35mm camera by Leica gave rise to a new breed of photographer, the photojournalists, now free to take their cameras anywhere. With a few 36-exposure films in their pocket, they photographed the world with a spontaneity never seen before.

Popularizing 35mm

The Leica 1, however, was expensive, and in the early 1930s Kodak mass-produced a much cheaper 35mm camera. It was this move that made 35mm the universally popular format that it is today. Despite what some people may have thought at the time, the large format cameras managed to survive this miniature revolution since, although the photojournalists opted for the smaller machines, professionals stuck to the larger negatives to reproduce nature and man-made objects as perfectly as possible. It was in the 1920s, 30s, and 40s that most of the great landscape pictures of America's West were made by photographic heroes like Edward Weston and Ansel Adams.

INTERNET

www.masters-of-photography.com/

This is a great web site for anybody who wants to see a small selection of works by some of the best photographers of all time. It includes pictures by Ansel Adams, Alfred Stieglitz, and Edward Weston, to name but a few.

Keeping things simple

THE MOST VERSATILE *and popular 35mm camera type available, the* SLR, *was launched in 1960. Its popularity has been largely due to the range of lenses and accessories available for it as well as its built-in electronic programming.*

DEFINITION

SLR *stands for single lens reflex and is a camera design in which the scene in the viewfinder is exactly the same as that "seen" by the lens. This is achieved by the use of an angled mirror and a series of silver surfaces.*

INSIDE AN SLR

The basic features – and the layout of those features – are the same in all 35mm SLRs, regardless of how different the cameras look.

Viewfinder window

Mirrored surfaces correct laterally reversed image from lens and direct light out through viewfinder

Light path through camera

Internal mirror corrects upside-down image from lens

Front lens elements

Shutter-speed dial

Film

Focal-plane shutter

Internal lens elements

Lens housing

But while the SLR was being launched and well received, the photographic industry was aware that millions of "ordinary people" wanted to take pictures without learning the comparatively complex techniques needed to use the SLR successfully.

Kodak, of course, was the first to offer the simple solution. The company introduced a 126 cartridge camera in 1963, the 110 cartridge in 1972, and, in 1982, they launched a disc camera. All these camera types were grouped together under the umbrella term "instamatics". The electronics were developing and these cameras were producing better exposed pictures in daylight and, with the introduction of an auto-flash unit, at night-time too. However, the quality was ultimately limited by the negative sizes, which were smaller than those from a 35mm film.

The modern compact

THE COMPACT CAMERA *as we know it today was launched in 1976 by Konica. This 35mm point-and-shoot was marketed with automatic focusing and exposure, as well as a built-in flash. Like all compacts for the next 4 years, this camera had a* fixed-focal-length lens *of 35mm. But in 1980 that all changed, when Minolta brought out the first compact with a zoom lens, offering a choice of two focal lengths, 38mm and 60mm. These days such cameras are called twin lens compacts.*

From that point on, the development of zoom lenses has exploded and compacts are now available with a variety of continuous zooms, such as 28–80mm, 35–70mm, and 35–105mm. Alongside the zoom boom came autoexposure and autofocus programming, fill-in automatic flash, remote shutter buttons, and all manner of other functions designed to make the non-technical photographer's life easier. The compact had come of age, making it possible to take excellent pictures without having to go to night school and without having to carry around a huge load of equipment.

■ **Compact cameras with zoom lenses** *were launched in 1980; zooms are now commonplace on even modestly priced point-and-shoots.*

The digital age

We're now experiencing the latest photography revolution. Although digital photography has been with us since the mid-1980s, it's only in the last couple of years that it has really been taken seriously.

Digital photography is the big leap; we've moved from recording images on light-sensitive emulsions to recording electronic images.

It's a logical progression out of the electronic technology that dominates every aspect of our lives. The general consensus in the industry is that traditional and electronic imaging will continue to co-exist for the next 30 years or so.

However, there's no doubt in my mind that the days of shooting on film and making a super darkroom print are numbered. It's a whole new world and we'll just have to wait and see what happens....

■ **If you're not** *familiar with digital cameras you may not even recognize this as one! They come in all shapes and sizes but basically do the same job as any other camera.*

A simple summary

✓ The first photograph was made in 1826 by Joseph Niepce.

✓ The negative-to-positive process was invented by William Fox Talbot in 1841.

✓ Early photography was an arduous process, but pioneering photographers were devoted to taking pictures of their world.

✓ By the early 1880s, instant exposures were available, leading to the invention of the shutter.

✓ In 1888, George Eastman founded the company Kodak.

✓ The first 35mm stills camera, the Leica 1, was unveiled in 1925.

✓ The SLR was launched in 1960. Within 3 years Kodak produced a simpler alternative.

✓ Konica produced the first 35mm compact camera in 1976.

✓ Digital photography's popularity has grown in the last few years.

Chapter 2

How the Camera Works

I LOVE THE FACT THAT NO MATTER HOW you look at a camera or how expensive it is, it's still basically a light-tight box with a film holder on one side and a lens opposite. Everything else has just been added on as extras. Imagine what a photographer of a hundred years ago would make of our all-singing, all-dancing cameras of the early 21st century. This chapter is all about the stuff we have added to make our cameras more accurate, lighter, sharper, and generally more convenient to use. It's about how these sophisticated machines work and how we stay in control of all that technology.

In this chapter...

✓ What is a camera?

✓ Camera basics

✓ The aperture–shutter marriage

✓ Exposing with the SLR system

LET'S FIND OUT WHY THE FOREGROUND IS SHARP AND THE BACKGROUND IS BLURRED

What is a camera?

THE BASIC CAMERA – and by that I mean every camera from the cheapest point-and-shoots to the newest and most complicated digital models – is a pinhole camera with other mechanical devices added to it.

You may have made a pinhole camera in science class at school. The pinhole camera is the most basic machine that can produce a photographic image. You remember the camera obscura that we discussed in the last chapter?

The pinhole camera is just a small version of the ancient camera obscura with, now that we have the chemistry, a sheet of film opposite the pinhole.

The image through the pinhole is projected on to the film upside-down and back to front. Because there's no lens, there's no way to focus the image, so it's not very sharp. However, the pinhole camera does produce a recognizable photographic picture of the subject.

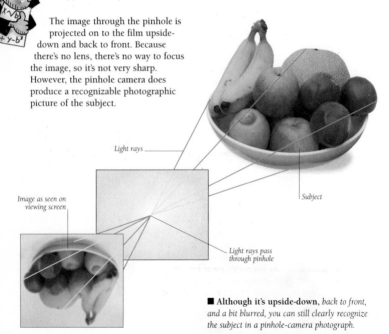

Light rays

Image as seen on viewing screen

Subject

Light rays pass through pinhole

■ **Although it's upside-down,** *back to front, and a bit blurred, you can still clearly recognize the subject in a pinhole-camera photograph.*

Camera basics

ON A "REAL" CAMERA, instead of a pinhole you have a lens, and a film holder keeps the film in place. The film is held a set distance from the lens so as to obtain a sharp image. There is also a film-transport system if the camera takes roll film, or a mechanism into which sheet-film magazines are inserted.

The lens must have a focus mechanism that moves it closer to or further from the film to ensure subjects that are, in turn, close or far from the lens, are kept sharp. The *aperture* of the lens is adjustable and is controlled by an *iris diaphragm*. The diaphragm controls the amount of light to which the film is exposed through the lens. A shutter is required to control the length of time the film is exposed to the light. There is also a viewfinder so that you, the photographer, can see what the camera "sees" through the lens.

DEFINITION

The diameter of a lens is called its **aperture**. *The adjustable mechanism of metal blades that forms the aperture is called an* **iris diaphragm**. *We'll keep things simple by calling the whole thing the aperture.*

INTERNET

www.pinholevisions.org/

Pinhole Visions is a great resource for those interested in pinhole photography. There is a fantastic gallery of pinhole photographs by a number of artists.

■ **As with a pinhole camera,** *the image that is captured on film in a conventional camera is still upside-down and back to front. However, the lens enables you to focus, the diaphragm controls the amount of light exposing the film, and the shutter allows you to control how long the film is exposed to the light. All this adds up to give you creative control.*

Subject

Lens

Diaphragm

Shutter

Viewfinder

Film

Aperture

The design of the aperture is based on the iris of the eye. You will have noticed that the iris of the eye opens when light is low and closes to a smaller diameter in bright light. Your lens aperture operates in the same way. The lens aperture is calculated on a

■ **This is how** the iris diaphragm works. The smaller the hole, or aperture, the less light is allowed through to expose the film.

scale of f-stops, or f-numbers, which are fractions of the focal length of the lens. So if you read on the front of your lens that it is a 50mm f2 lens, it means that the maximum aperture is *half* the focal length of the lens; in this case, 25 mm (50÷2). Because f-stops are fractions, the larger the f-number, the smaller the aperture, and vice versa.

The term "to stop down" is universally used to mean the closing down of the aperture to a smaller diameter. To open up means to increase the aperture to a larger diameter.

Increasing the aperture by 1 stop (this is achieved on SLR cameras by the use of an "aperture ring") doubles the volume of light entering through the lens. Decreasing by 1 stop halves the light allowed to enter. So, for example, if you stop down from f5.6 to f8 (this is 1 stop), you halve the volume of light entering through the lens, and if you open up 1 stop from f5.6 to f4, you double the volume of light entering through the lens. This can all be rather confusing, but once you get to grips with the fact that f-stops are fractions then it will start to make sense and be easier to remember.

Many aperture rings also have half-stop positions – for example, an aperture position halfway between f5.6 and f8.

The aperture controls the depth of focus of a lens.

Focusing ring ──

Aperture ring ──

DEFINITION

The depth of focus is the distance in front and behind your picture's main subject that is also kept sharply focused. It's also sometimes called depth of field.

■ **Adjustments to focusing** and aperture are made through the use of rings round the lens.

Don't just snap away at your subject without considering the depth of focus.

Your lens has a depth-of-focus scale that tells you how much depth of focus you get at each f-stop. Further to this, many SLR cameras have a stop-down button. This allows you to see the amount of depth you get as you stop down.

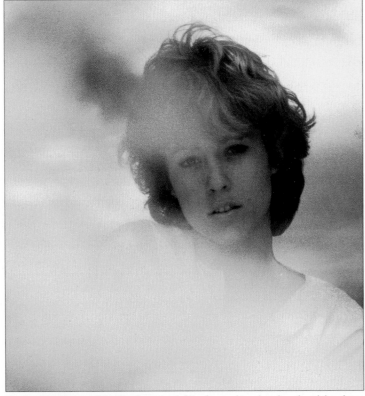

■ **I shot this picture** *at f2.8 with a shutter speed of ½₂₅₀ of a second in order to keep the girl sharp but blur both the foreground and background.*

■ **To increase your depth of field** *try stopping right down and using a slow shutter speed. For this picture I set the aperture to f16 and the shutter to ⅓₀ of a second.*

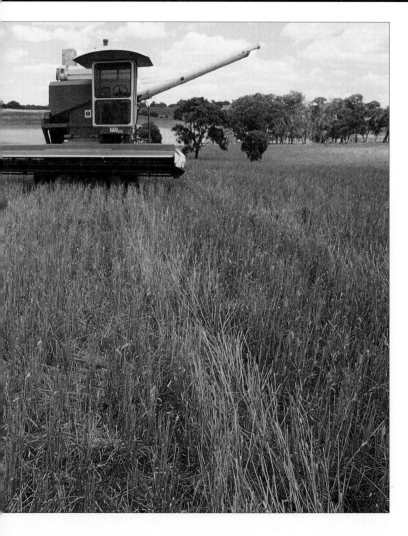

Shutter

As I mentioned in Chapter 1, the shutter is the camera mechanism that controls the length of time for which light is allowed to expose the film. There are basically two different designs of shutter mechanisms: the leaf shutter and the focal-plane shutter.

 The leaf shutter This is of a similar structure to the aperture – a series of overlapping metal leaves that open and close to expose the film. The leaf shutter is built into the lens and is used mostly on large format cameras.

 The focal-plane shutter Almost universal in SLR cameras, the focal-plane shutter is basically a curtain with a slit that travels across the film plane exposing the film. Some designs use two curtains. The focal-plane shutter is positioned at the back of the camera, in front of the film.

TYPICAL SLR SHUTTER-SPEED SEQUENCE

Shutter speeds are in fractions of a second. In all SLR models, electronic shutters now provide speeds from an incredible $\frac{1}{8000}$ of a second up to 30 seconds. When setting shutter speeds manually, every change up to a faster speed or change down to the next slow speed has the same exposure consequence as opening up or stopping down the aperture by 1 stop. Changing from $\frac{1}{250}$ of a second to $\frac{1}{125}$ of a second doubles the length of time for which the light exposes the film, and, of course, when you change from $\frac{1}{250}$ of a second to $\frac{1}{500}$ of a second you halve the length of time that the light exposes the film.

- 1 second
- $\frac{1}{2}$ second
- $\frac{1}{4}$ of a second
- $\frac{1}{8}$ of a second
- $\frac{1}{15}$ of a second
- $\frac{1}{30}$ of a second
- $\frac{1}{60}$ of a second
- $\frac{1}{125}$ of a second
- $\frac{1}{250}$ of a second
- $\frac{1}{500}$ of a second
- $\frac{1}{1000}$ of a second
- $\frac{1}{2000}$ of a second
- $\frac{1}{4000}$ of a second

■ **The range of shutter speeds** *varies between cameras. Yours may have fewer or more options than this example.*

RELEASING THE SHUTTER

When the shutter is in its closed position, not only does the film remain hidden from light but also a mirror reflects the light up to the viewfinder. When you press the shutter-release button, the shutter opens and the mirror lifts out of the way.

BEFORE SHUTTER RELEASE   DURING SHUTTER RELEASE

The aperture–shutter marriage

SO LET'S SUM UP THE BASICS. *The aperture is the diameter of the lens, through which light exposes the film. By increasing and decreasing the size of the aperture (making a bigger or smaller hole), you control the volume of light entering the camera. The shutter is the mechanism that opens and closes to control the length of time the light is exposing the film. The aperture and the shutter are totally wedded together, and one cannot be altered without the other being altered also.*

I will explain this because it's important that you understand the relationship between the two. However, in practical terms most of the rest of this chapter is only relevant to SLR users. Compact, or point-and-shoot, cameras are automated – the camera does all the calculations – and their users are not able to control their cameras to the same degree as SLR users. However, it is worth knowing the theory so I urge you to continue reading this chapter. (We will look at the point-and-shoot camera in detail in Part Two.)

Reading your light meter

When you take a light reading, using either the **TTL metering** on your SLR camera or a separate hand-held light meter, the meter gives you a range of alternative settings, each of which is an average "correct" exposure. That means that each alternative lets in the same amount of light. Point-and-shoot cameras also make exposure readings but the user doesn't know what combination of shutter speed and aperture the camera has chosen. (However, the expensive, top-of-the-range point-and-shoots – called super-compacts – do give you a choice of aperture combinations.)

> [DEFINITION]
>
> **TTL metering** is through-the-lens light metering.

The light meter (whether built-in or separate) takes a reading of the amount of light reflecting off your subject. But to get the correct exposure combination you also have to tell the meter what speed (ISO rating) of film you have in the camera.

■ **This diagram** *shows a series of six aperture–shutter settings. Each aperture setting is wedded to the shutter speed beneath it. Every one of these six combinations lets in the same volume of light.*

How do I choose my shutter speed?

Each aperture–shutter speed combination in the list below is a correct exposure according to the sample meter reading alongside.

Aperture	Shutter speed
f2.8	$\frac{1}{1000}$ of a second
f4	$\frac{1}{500}$ of a second
f5.6	$\frac{1}{250}$ of a second
f8	$\frac{1}{125}$ of a second
f11	$\frac{1}{60}$ of a second
f16	$\frac{1}{30}$ of a second

SAMPLE METER READING

So... which combination to use? Does it matter? You bet it does! But in order to make this choice you need to know what other properties the aperture and shutter possess.

You already know that the aperture controls the depth of focus of the lens. The smaller the aperture, the greater the depth of focus; the larger the aperture, the smaller the depth of focus.

Well, the shutter controls movement in the photograph, or rather it controls the degree of sharpness or blur that a moving object makes across the frame of your picture. A fast shutter speed – like $\frac{1}{1000}$ of a second – will freeze a cyclist whizzing past the camera, while on $\frac{1}{30}$ of second, the cyclist will appear blurred.

Most unintentionally out-of-focus pictures are caused by camera shake. Shutter speeds must be fast enough to prevent camera shake.

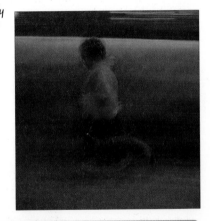

■ **By selecting** *a slow shutter speed when action is moving quickly past you, the effect in the resulting picture will be a blurred image.*

COMBATING CAMERA SHAKE

The longer the lens you have on your camera, the more camera shake you will experience. To reduce the effect of camera shake, your shutter speed needs to increase in line with the focal length of your lens. Use this guide to cut down your blur.

Focal length	Shutter speed
● 24–35mm	$\frac{1}{30}$ of a second
● 50mm	$\frac{1}{60}$ of a second
● 105mm	$\frac{1}{125}$ of a second
● 200mm	$\frac{1}{250}$ of a second
● 500mm	$\frac{1}{500}$ of a second

Exposing with the SLR system

THE EXPOSURE-METERING SYSTEM *of the modern SLR camera is incredibly sophisticated. Most SLRs work either on automatic or manual. Although the metering systems can solve most problems, they are useless unless you know how they do what they do, and you have to know what result you want. As with a computer, cameras can only do the job well if you give them the right instructions.*

I cannot emphasize enough how important it is to study your instruction book thoroughly. Each camera has slightly different systems and I can only talk here in general terms. Always keep your instruction book in your camera bag.

The exposure-metering systems

There are three different metering methods and many SLR cameras incorporate all three. Let's look at each of them.

Centre-weighted metering

Centre-weighted metering is fairly self-descriptive. The reading is taken from the control area of the viewfinder (usually a 12-mm diameter area). This is the first system used by SLR cameras and is an excellent all-round metering system. You can move the camera around the picture area, make a decision about which area is most important, and set the exposure accordingly.

CENTRE-WEIGHTED METERING

Matrix metering

This is a sophisticated computer meter. The meter's computer has been fed the exposure values of about 100,000 sample photographs. Each photograph is of a different subject in differing light conditions. With this knowledge at its disposal, the meter can make an accurate exposure calculation on any subject and lighting conditions put before it. The exposure reading is taken from the whole of the picture area. The viewfinder is divided up into

MATRIX METERING

segments, each of which is metered before the computer evaluates the results and makes a decision. Matrix is an ideal system to use before you are confident of your technique. Theoretically, because of its 100,000-picture memory, it can read and solve all the traditional exposure problems such as back-lighting. However, in my experience, the matrix system is not infallible and I prefer using spot metering for tricky situations.

Spot metering

Not all SLR cameras have a spot meter, but most of the latest mid- to top-of-the-range models do. The spot meter takes a reading from a circular area of (depending on the camera) 3–5mm in diameter in the middle of the viewfinder. (It uses approximately 2–2½ per cent of the viewfinder's area.) By pointing the spot at any area of the picture you can take a precise reading of an area that you consider critical, like the focal point perhaps. Spot metering is perfect for difficult situations like a small (in the frame), brightly lit face in front of a dark

SPOT METERING

background, or the reverse, with a small, dark object against a very light background. You'll find that you use spot metering more and more as you get more experienced.

Many professionals use spot metering for landscapes. They take a series of highlight and shadow readings before making a decision on which is more important. Or they may decide an average is more desirable. They then set the aperture and shutter combination manually.

Aperture priority and shutter priority

Some SLRs set the exposure by the aperture priority method – that is, you set the aperture and the camera automatically sets the correct shutter speed – and some use shutter priority, in which you select the shutter speed and the camera chooses the correct aperture. Most of the top-of-the-range cameras offer both methods.

I don't believe both are required, because by altering the shutter speed you get the aperture you require for your considered depth of focus. Alternatively, by changing your aperture you can find the shutter speed you want if movement control (not forgetting camera shake) is a critical factor. Each system is as good as the other.

■ **You can alter** *the aperture setting on your SLR camera simply by turning the aperture ring that you'll find on the lens.*

Exposure compensation

An SLR camera has another method for fine-tuning exposure called exposure compensation. Many top-of-the-range point-and-shoots – and not just super-compacts – also incorporate exposure compensation. Some cameras have a dial at the top of the camera body with a scale reading -2 -1 0 +1 +2, while fully electronic cameras display this scale in the LCD when you push the appropriate button (see your instruction book for more in-depth information). Exposure compensation allows the photographer to override the autoexposure and over- or underexpose the film by up to 2 stops in steps of ⅓ of a stop.

INTERNET

www.betterphoto.com/
exploring/groenhout
Exposure.asp

This web page is well worth visiting: it contains an interesting article called "Obtaining Correct Exposure".

■ **You can override** *the automatic exposure on your SLR and over- or underexpose your film by using the exposure compensation.*

If you have been using exposure compensation, never pack away the camera without first making sure the control is set back to 0. Otherwise you could pull the camera out and accidentally over- or underexpose your next picture.

Exposure compensation is useful when you want creative control of your exposure – when you want to give a different exposure to the one that the auto setting has come up with. Some cameras (including some point-and-shoots) have a back-light button that increases the exposure by 1½ stops to compensate for the fact that the light pouring straight into the meter through the lens has fooled the lens into underexposing the foreground. The exposure-compensation function does the same thing. I use it for back-lighting: at +1½ stops it does the same as a back-light button. I also use exposure compensation when filtering black-and-white film. I go +1 or +1½ stops to make sure that the increased contrast produced by the filter does not leave the shadows underexposed.

When in their fully automated modes, most point-and-shoots will automatically balance the back-light by using a flash fill.

■ **Strong back-light in a scene** *fools the camera's light meter into underexposing the film. I used +1 exposure compensation for this picture to prevent the back-light from ruining the shot.*

SLR programs

Yet another exposure system built into most SLR cameras is called programming. With programmed exposure control, the computer automatically adjusts the aperture and shutter speed to the correct exposure.

To describe programming, I will use the system on my Nikon 90X as an example. Your camera will vary in its programming but the principle is the same.

There are two main programs: the fully automatic Auto Multi Program (P on the LCD screen), which is designed to select shutter and aperture settings for "average" subjects and is high enough to avoid camera shake, and the Vari Program (PS on LCD), which is more flexible and has the following subprograms.

PO Portrait program

Sets the largest aperture for the available exposure value to enable the subject to stand out against a blurred (out-of-focus) background.

HF Hyperfocal program

Stops down the aperture to keep both the foreground and background sharp.

LP Landscape program

Stops down the aperture for maximum foreground-to-infinity depth of focus.

SL Silhouette program

Underexposes a foreground subject against a brightly lit background – for example, a sunset – to make it into a silhouette.

SP Sports program

Selects the fastest possible shutter speed for the lighting conditions in order to freeze the movement.

CU Close-up program

Exposes for close-up shots and ignores the background.

Now these programs may sound great but in my opinion they only complicate one's photographic life – and all of them are compromises. I recommend that you use the other systems and learn to make your own decisions. You take the pictures – don't let the manufacturers control your creative decisions.

A simple summary

✓ Every camera available to buy is basically a glorified version of a pinhole camera. However, instead of a pinhole there is a lens, and the viewed image is recorded on to a piece of film.

✓ The diameter of a lens is called its aperture. Lens aperture is adjusted by the use of an iris diaphragm to let more or less light into the camera.

✓ Aperture is measured as an f-stop, or f-number, which is a fraction of the lens's focal length. The larger the f-number, the smaller the aperture.

✓ The shutter controls the length of time for which the film inside the camera is exposed to light.

✓ Aperture and shutter work together. If one is altered, the other must be too.

✓ A light meter will give you several aperture–shutter choices, but to make a correct exposure you must also tell the meter what speed film you are using.

✓ The same amount of light will expose the film in any one of several aperture–shutter combinations.

✓ There are three different SLR exposure-metering systems: centre-weighted, matrix, and spot metering.

✓ Your camera may expose by aperture priority or by shutter priority. In each case, you select one setting and the camera automatically adjusts the other.

✓ Exposure compensation is useful when you want a different exposure setting to that which the camera has selected.

✓ Many SLRs also have an exposure program system that contains appropriate settings for certain types of photography.

Chapter 3

Which Camera to Choose?

CHOOSING WHICH CAMERA to buy can feel like walking through a minefield. The advertising hype confuses the issue considerably. We can defuse the problem by asking ourselves a few simple questions. This chapter suggests what those questions might be for you and helps you formulate a sensible and cost-effective answer.

In this chapter...

✓ What camera should I buy?

✓ But I like my current camera...

✓ In simple terms

A GOOD SUBJECT SHOT WELL WILL MAKE A GOOD PICTURE REGARDLESS OF THE CAMERA YOU USE

What camera should I buy?

THIS IS A VERY DIFFICULT *question to advise on. Over the years I have had hundreds of friends and acquaintances ask me that very thing. I would guess that almost all of you who have bought this book have probably got at least one camera of some sort at home, so what we're really talking about is what camera to buy next.*

I think I can be most helpful by asking you a few questions first. The first, and probably the most important, point to get out of the way is "What's your budget?" I need to jump in here and say that cameras have never been as cheap as they are now. When you consider wages and inflation, cameras cost about half what they did in the early 1970s. Even a fairly small budget can get you a surprisingly good camera.

■ **It can all seem** *pretty complicated out there in the camera shops. Even after you've decided which type to buy, there is still a huge range to choose from.*

What are my needs?

Once you've decided how much you want (or can afford) to spend, you need to consider what you'll be using your camera for. Ask yourself the following questions:

1) **What do I want to photograph?** This is an important question. For example, if you are about to go on a safari holiday and are hoping to take some great pictures of the African wildlife, you should immediately discount a point-and-shoot camera. You just couldn't get the sort of intimate, close-up shots that you would undoubtedly want to capture in such a phenomenal setting. For photography such as this, only a 35mm SLR camera with a long lens (or two) will suffice. If you want to take some pictures of your newborn child and continue to do so as he or she grows up, however, an APS camera might provide the perfect solution.

2) **Will I be the only person using it?** The reason you need to ask yourself this is because, if the answer is no, you will need to bear in mind the needs of the other users in terms of both camera capabilities and simplicity of use. You may be the world's biggest technophile, but maybe the others users are not. Most point-and-shoot cameras offer a choice between total automation and the user having some degree of control, so this might be a good choice for multiple users.

3 **Am I more interested in technique or creativity?** The basics of photographic technique are applicable to all cameras and as such even a cheap compact will offer some practice opportunities. Regarding creativity, you can, of course, be creative with a point-and-shoot camera through your choice of subjects, but if you want to maximize your creative control over the images you produce you need to consider a fully manual 35mm SLR. However, if your creative input is going to come at a later stage, using a computer after the picture has been taken, you might want to consider going digital from the start.

4 **What will I do with the images I produce?** There are many different options here: you may want to e-mail them to friends and family, make huge prints to decorate the inside walls of your home, or document your daily life, for example. I would suggest digital, 35mm SLR, and either APS or point-and-shoot cameras respectively.

But I like my current camera...

IF YOU ALREADY HAVE A CAMERA

that you love to bits and you are happy with the results it gives you, don't be bullied into buying a new all-singing, all-dancing model. Knowing your camera is a vitally important part of producing creative work.

■ **Buying a new camera** *doesn't mean you have to throw away your old one. Why not keep it as a back-up?*

On the other hand, though, you might want to take advantage of some of the new technologies, like autofocus and improved zoom lenses. There are some great budget models available now that are aimed at the keen amateur – many are even of suitable specification for professionals. Or, if you have a point-and-shoot, you may feel that you would like a little (or a lot) more creative freedom, in which case why not get an SLR, and keep your much-loved compact as a second camera?

There are some real brand-new camera bargains out there, but you could also consider buying second-hand from a camera shop that you trust.

In simple terms

OKAY, LET'S GET DOWN to the nitty-gritty. I'm going to give you a brief, simple breakdown of which cameras are best for which people. Of course, this list can only be in general terms: you might feel you don't quite fit into any of these categories, or that you fit into more than one. Please use this list as a guideline; only you know what you want from your new camera.

Computer-minded

If you are a computer expert, you may enjoy manipulating your pictures using Photoshop® on your computer before printing them out. Or you might want to e-mail images to your family and friends. If that sounds like you, I would be inclined to say, "Go digital". The prices of digital equipment are higher than those of conventional gear but they're coming down fast... and you won't have to pay for developing ever again.

No hassle required

If you are looking for the simplest, most hassle-free camera, go for an APS point-and-shoot. Although they are tiny, the quality of image is pretty good (but not as good as on a 35mm point-and-shoot because the negative is half the size). If you follow my tips on composition and light, you will be able to use your creative eye to produce some exciting photographs. I also think an APS is worth considering as a second camera if you already have an SLR you are happy with.

Don't fall for the APS as a fashion accessory. They may look good but is that what you really need photographically?

■ **APS cameras** *offer a no-hassle option. It's possible to take some great pictures, and if you want a reprint, you select it from your index print – no more trawling through negatives!*

Quality and convenience

If you want better quality than APS offers, go for a 35mm compact with either a fixed or zoom lens. A fixed-lens compact usually has a wide-angle lens of 28mm, 32mm, or 35mm. These cameras are nearly as small as APS cameras and can produce good pictures. The quality of the lens and the strength of the flash improve as the price goes up. If you are going for a zoom-lens compact, don't buy one that is too telephoto; the maximum aperture at the 135mm end of a point-and-shoot zoom is about f11 to f16, which is pretty useless, so don't go over 105mm. Play around with the camera for a while. The feel and balance is very important. Choose a camera that feels comfortable in your hand. I would strongly advise you not to buy loads of modes that you don't need – they will cost extra. There are also some super-compacts available that have superb lenses, both manual and auto. They are made as snap cameras for professionals and can set you back as much as £1,000.

Getting serious

If you mean to get serious about your photography there is no doubt in my mind that you need a 35mm SLR camera. The 35mm is incredibly versatile and, in the right hands, can produce images of a stunning quality. SLRs have an enormous range of lenses and accessories that will allow a photographer to shoot almost anything at all. My lenses range from 15mm to 1000mm.

When buying new lenses check out the specialist companies, like Sigma. They offer good quality at nearly half the price of some other manufacturers.

If you're buying a good SLR, you should also purchase a strong, light tripod at the same time. Tripods add that extra option for the serious photographer – the chance to look at the long-shutter-speed world.

■ **Armed with** *a 35mm SLR, a telephoto lens, and a few filters, the world is your oyster.*

BUILDING UP YOUR EQUIPMENT

For those of you who are thinking about going SLR, here is a list of recommended equipment that you can build up in stages.

Stage 1

- Camera body
- Waterproof camera bag
- 28–70mm zoom
- Polarizing filter
- Orange filter
- Red filter (for black-and-white work)
- Tripod

Stage 2

- 80–200mm zoom
- Flashgun with extension cord

CAMERA BAG AND TRIPOD

Stage 3

- 20mm wide-angle lens
- Large aperture 50mm f1.4 lens, for photography where flash isn't possible
- Underwater compact for beach holidays

UNDERWATER COMPACT CAMERA

If you can't afford an underwater compact, buy a handful of underwater single-use cameras whenever you go on a beach holiday. They are literally point-and-shoot, but the results are often great!

Stage 4

- A good point-and-shoot, for those occasions when you don't want to take all your kit but an important picture opportunity may come up

When you are looking to buy a brand-new camera it's important to keep an eye on the product reviews in photography magazines. The reviewers are experienced photographers, so take advantage of their advice.

Do haggle when you are buying a new camera. The salesperson might throw in a bag of filters or some other useful accessories to secure your custom.

INTERNET

www.camerareview.com

This is a great place to start if you're not sure which SLR camera to buy. You can even type in what features you're looking for, and they'll come back with a list of cameras that fit the bill.

A simple summary

✓ The first thing to consider when buying a camera is your budget.

✓ Cameras are less expensive now than they have ever been.

✓ Once your budget is decided, four other points need to be considered: what you'll use the camera for, whether you'll be the sole user, how creative you want to be, and what you'll do with your resulting images.

✓ If your old camera works just fine and you know how to get the best out of it, keep it, even if you do buy a new one.

✓ Going digital is worth considering if you want to manipulate your images or e-mail them to people.

✓ If you want a hassle-free life, an APS is a good choice.

✓ A 35mm compact offers better print quality than an APS, and it's not that much bigger.

✓ If you really want to maximize your creative-photography potential, get a 35mm SLR.

✓ Camera reviews in photography magazines are invaluable sources of advice for buyers.

Chapter 4

Film

SELECTING A FILM is just about as confusing as choosing which camera to buy next. The advertisers tell us that this brand is better than that one and, if we were to take too much notice, we might believe that we could never take a good picture without their product. The truth is that there are no poor-quality films on the market. Let's see what it's all about.

In this chapter...

✓ Film choices

✓ Film speed

✓ Colour print film

✓ Colour slide film

✓ Black-and-white film

✓ Specialist films

YOU DON'T NEED COLOUR FILM TO CREATE ATMOSPHERIC SHOTS

Film choices

BRAND NAME isn't the most important consideration in choosing film – so what is? Before you can make a choice you need to know what's available. The three main groups of film are **colour negative** (or print film), colour positive (or slide film), and black-and-white film. (When talking about black-and-white we are almost always referring to negative film.)

ROLL OF 35MM FILM

> **DEFINITION**
>
> **Colour negative** film produces a negative, or reverse, image from which your print is made. You will hear people refer to colour negative film as print film.

Don't buy old film even if it's on special offer – it's simply not worth the risk. As with everything else in the supermarket, check the sell-by date on the packet.

To help you decide which group of films to choose from, we will look at each of them in detail, but first of all I'm going to teach you all about film speed.

Film speed

THE TERM FILM SPEED is one of the most used bits of photographic jargon, and it refers to a film's sensitivity to light: the faster the film, the more sensitive it is to light. A fast film, therefore, requires less light than a slow film to produce a photographic image.

Film speed is calculated in ISO ratings, and you can buy film from as slow as 25 ISO right up to as fast as 3200 ISO, which can in turn be *pushed* up to 25000 ISO – I'll move on to that in a minute.

> **DEFINITION**
>
> ISO is simply an abbreviation for International Standards Organization. Some of your older cameras and books will have an ASA rating. ASA ratings are exactly the same as ISO ratings. The term **pushing** means to expose a film to less light than its ISO rating dictates. You need to tell your lab if you do this because they will have to develop the film differently. Pushing is sometimes also known as uprating.

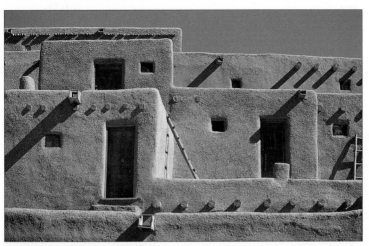

■ **A slow film (100 ISO) was ideal** *for the detail in Adobe House, New Mexico. It's hard to see in this small space, but the 35mm negative enlarges to 40 x 50 cm (16 x 20 in), pin sharp and almost grain-free.*

As a general rule of thumb, the slower the film, the smaller the grain and the sharper the image. Contrast is also related to film speed – the slower the film, the higher the contrast. Also, when specifically discussing colour, the slower the film, the more saturated the colour will be. It follows, then, that the faster the film, the grainier it is, and the softer its contrast, colour, and sharpness.

Films have their ISO ratings on the box, and they usually start at 100 ISO with 200 ISO, 400 ISO, 800 ISO, and 1600 ISO following. ISO ratings are in logical relative steps, so a 200 ISO film is twice as sensitive to light as a 100 ISO and requires half the volume of light to produce a satisfactory image.

■ **Here I used a fast slide film** *pushed even faster (1600 ISO pushed to 3200 ISO) for a soft, grainy effect. I was trying to get the feel of an Impressionist painting.*

Everyday choice

Before we go into any great depth, I'll stick my neck out here and strongly advise you to make 400 ISO film your standard purchase regardless of which type of film you are using. I say this because it's fast enough to cope with most light situations and the grain structure has become much finer recently. Another benefit of 400 ISO as standard is that it's fast enough to reduce the effects of camera shake, which is the most common cause of out-of-focus pictures.

If you are using telephoto lenses, use a fast film – 400 ISO or faster – because camera shake is magnified by telephoto lenses. Fast films allow for faster shutter speeds, which in turn overcome camera shake. Or you could use a tripod of course.

Pushing and pulling

To push a film you need to increase the film speed at which the camera is operating. This is usually done either with a dial, which you will probably find on the top of your camera, or via a menu system. Ordinarily, this setting should correlate to the ISO rating of the film you are using. Check your camera's instruction manual if you can't find the control. Such trickery, unfortunately, is not possible on a compact, or point-and-shoot, camera.

MANUAL SLR DIAL

Just to complicate things slightly, film speed is also related to development. Increasing the development time from normal has the same effect as increasing the ISO rating, and both methods are known as pushing.

Never change your camera's ISO setting in the middle of a film. Some of the film will be well exposed and some won't.

Professional photographers have been pushing their films for years. There are two reasons for this:

1. To obtain a satisfactory image when the lighting is too low for the film being used

2. To take advantage of the increased grain size to produce a painterly effect

Pushing film also results in increased contrast. Recently, new chemical technology has resulted in a breed of special push films. These films have an ISO rating as normal but are designed to be processed at an extra 2–2½ stops, so an 800 ISO film could be developed as though it were a 4800 ISO film. This greatly increases the contrast and grain size.

Before you buy push film, make sure that your minilab does a push service. If not find a local pro lab.

It's important to grasp the point that the pushing of a film from 400 ISO to 600 ISO is the equivalent of opening up the aperture half a stop, and pushing from 400 ISO to 800 ISO is equal to opening up 1 stop.

Try to use the correct terminology when talking to your lab – they will take you more seriously. If you want your 400 ISO pushed to 800 ISO tell them you want it pushed 1 stop.

Pulling film down from the rated speed to a slower ISO rating is also possible but, unless you have mistakenly shot a 400 ISO film at 200 ISO and need to compensate in development, I don't think there's any point in pulling film. You may as well use a slower film and cash in on its properties – the finer grain and increased colour saturation.

Keep a permanent marker pen in your bag so that you can immediately write down the ISO rating to which you pushed the film on the canister or the film itself as soon as you remove it.

By all means experiment with pushing and pulling films. But I highly recommend that you use the special push films. Don't miss out if your supermarket (or wherever you buy your film) doesn't stock them, find a professional camera shop in the nearest big city to you and get hold of some. The quality is even better than the general range.

Never throw an exposed film into your bag thinking you will mark it later – you will forget and ruin a great film.

■ **It's important** to mark a pushed film as soon as you remove it from the camera. If you pushed a 400 ISO by 1 stop – for example – mark it 800 ISO.

Grain

The light-sensitive photographic emulsion on film is formed by silver crystals, and it's these crystals that give a grainy texture to your images. In order for a fast film to catch more light quicker than a slow film, the silver crystals (and therefore the grains on the photographs) are larger. A slow film is coated with smaller crystals. The slow film's small grain size makes for a less grainy effect and also allows for a higher resolution because the image is not being broken up by the larger grain structure of fast film. Some photographers hate grain and others love it.

Most professionals don't agree with the film speeds quoted by the manufacturers. For maximum quality at normal development I would rate 400 ISO at 320 on my meter and 200 ISO at 125.

■ **Although I didn't need** *a fast film to obtain a satisfactory exposure, I used a 1000 ISO pushed to 2500 (2¼ stops). It was a creative decision. I visualized soft, merging colours, rather than the clean, hard-edged colours that a 100 or 200 ISO film would have given me. My romantic period... or something! Note the large grain structure in the detail.*

In real life, however, unless you are making a *blow-up* larger than 10 x 8 inches (25 x 20 cm), you will notice very little difference in grain size between 100 ISO and 800 ISO film on your prints.

If you want to experiment with grainy pictures you need to find a custom lab – as used by professionals – and discuss technique with them. Severe push development of fast film is the usual method.

Very grainy colour can have a lovely romantic atmosphere similar to an Impressionist painting. Grainy black-and-white looks like an old etching.

■ **This still life required** a very different film choice to that used opposite. My wife Michelle used a very slow (50 ISO) transparency film to get the ultimate in colour saturation, fine grain, and sharpness. This time in the detail, note how fine the grain structure is.

Colour print film

IT'S LIKELY THAT THE MAJORITY of newcomers to photography will be used to using colour print film, and it's for this reason that I'll deal with it first of the film types.

Colour print films have improved greatly over the last 10 years. They're sharper, have finer grain, and are capable of better colour rendition. In fact, it's the improvement in print film that has made the APS possible.

The APS negative is almost half the size of a full 35mm negative, so it needs the new high-quality films in order to produce a good print.

> **DEFINITION**
>
> **Exposure latitude** is the amount a film can be under- or overexposed and still produce a satisfactory print.

The advantage of print film over slide film is its *exposure latitude*. Print film can be under- or overexposed by 2 stops and still produce a reasonable print. This means that the camera's metering system doesn't need to be very accurate, which is why you can achieve remarkably good results with cheap point-and-shoot cameras. It's this latitude that has led to sports and press photographers turning to colour print film recently.

The colour print film processing system is called the C41 process.

Print film is far more tolerant to tungsten and other artificial light than slide film. It's even possible to correct at the printing stage a colour cast that has been recorded on the negative. Also, there are warm- and cool-tone films on the market, so you can choose whether to go for natural subtle colours or very saturated colours.

■ **I have chosen** *a negative with a full range of colours so that you can see, by comparing it to the print, how colours look in negative form. You'll see that they are the opposites of each other: the greens of the negative print as reds, for example.*

THE PRINT

THE NEGATIVE

Colour slide film

MOST PROFESSIONAL PHOTOGRAPHERS *still use* **transparency** *film for their colour work. The reason for this is that you can control the result in the camera. You are not reliant on a printer or an automatic printing machine for your results. Transparencies are the ultimate in colour quality.*

If you are a point-and-shoot user, I'm afraid that the next couple of pages are going to be of academic interest only to you, because the compact camera's exposure system is built with print film in mind. The metering is not sufficiently accurate to deal with the lack of exposure latitude that slide film offers.

SLIDE

MOUNTED SLIDE

> *Exposure is subjective and relative to your visualization of a subject. One person's "correct" exposure may look overexposed to somebody else.*

If you are after a dark, moody image you can underexpose the transparency film without worrying that a printing machine will compensate for the underexposure and try to produce a "correctly exposed" print. You have much more creative control.

If you used a colour-correction filter to change the colour balance of a scene, you would know that what you see in the viewfinder is how the transparency is going to look – without the interference of a printing machine.

> *An automatic printing machine is designed to produce an average, or normal, print, which may not be what you want creatively.*

Trivia...

Slide film is distinguished by the word "chrome" at the end of the trade name – for example, Kodachrome, Ektachrome, Fujichrome, Agfachrome. Colour print film has "color" (note the US spelling) at the end.

Bracketing

When shooting on slide film, most professionals *bracket* their exposures. The reasons for this are two-fold:

1 If you are being paid lots of money to take a picture, you can't afford to risk an exposure mistake

2 A shot that is under- or overexposed (by the meter's calculation) can sometimes have a great look to it that the photographer didn't visualize through the viewfinder

I would strongly advise you to bracket your exposures whenever it's practical to do so – when shooting landscapes and still lifes, for example.

Never bracket exposures on unrepeatable subjects like sports or children playing because the best shot could be the one that is over- or underexposed.

DEFINITION

*To **bracket** exposures means to take a series of exposures both under and over the meter reading. With your SLR you will most probably have an exposure compensation facility that allows you to go up or down 2 stops in ⅓-of-a-stop increments.*

The clip test

Another safety procedure is to have your lab process a *clip test*. If the test is a bit light or dark you can ask the lab to adjust the remaining film and development accordingly. You need to find a good custom lab for this sort of service.

DEFINITION

*A **clip test** is a short piece of film – about three frames – cut off the start of the film and developed, to check that your exposures are perfect.*

The film manufacturers produce both a professional line and an amateur line of slide film. Check out the pro films, they are superior. A recent development has been the introduction of warm-tone and cool-tone emulsions. The cool tones are more suitable for skin tones and the warm tones are more suitable for producing saturated, vibrant colours.

Don't use warm-tone films for portrait work. The skin tones can have a magenta cast.

When using slide film in tungsten light, it's important to remember that you need to use tungsten-balanced slide film. Daylight slide film will go reddish in tungsten light. You can, however, shoot with daylight film and correct it with an *80B filter*. Or filter your tungsten lights with 80B filters!

DEFINITION

*An **80B filter** is a blue filter that restores the colour temperature of tungsten light back to daylight.*

Trivia...

Many pros are obsessive about clip testing and will have their films pushed or pulled about ¼ of a stop after inspecting the clip. Too small a margin for the average amateur to notice.

The slide show

Finally, call me an old romantic, but you haven't really seen colour photography if you've never seen a slide show. Slides projected on to a big screen look fantastic; I still project mine and add some background music. Slides can be made into great prints too. Although it's a bit more expensive, you do have the slide as a guide for your print quality.

Colour transparency film is called colour reversal film by the manufacturers because it is first processed as a negative and is then re-exposed halfway through the process. The re-exposure reverses the image to a transparency, which is a positive image.

Black-and-white film

I WILL BE DISCUSSING *the visualization of our colourful world into tones of black-and-white in Chapter 22; in this section I am simply telling you about the black-and-white films that are available and suggesting which films work best in different circumstances. To get the most out of black-and-white photography ideally you need to be developing and printing your own stuff – the great joy of black-and-white is watching that printed image magically appear in the developing dish. But if you're new to photography that's all in the future... or you may decide to leave it to somebody else.*

THE NEGATIVE

THE PRINT

Black-and-white photography has had a big revival lately and the manufacturers have responded by producing what are called **chromogenic** black-and-white films. These films can be processed by minilabs using the C41 (colour print film) chemistry rather than the conventional black-and-white processing that needs more individual attention.

> **DEFINITION**
>
> **Chromogenic** *means "as colour"* – chrom(os) *being Greek for colour. These films are black-and-whites that can be processed and printed in the same way as colour film.*

Film manufacturers Kodak®, Konica, and Ilford all produce chromogenic black-and-white films.

Chromogenic films are great for you to experiment with to see if you like black-and-white.

Chromogenic films have a dye image rather than the silver crystal image of conventional black-and-white film.

Conventional black-and-white films have a huge range of ISO ratings from 25 ISO to 3200 ISO, which can be processed up to 25000 ISO. I would strongly recommend you find a good custom lab specializing in black-and-white printing before you start experimenting with conventional black-and-white films though, otherwise the prints might be disappointing and a bit of a turn-off.

INTERNET

www.apogeephoto.com/
buyguide/index1.htm

Click on "Film" for a selection of film manufacturers; for each one there's a detailed product guide.

■ **The rain** *was coming down and the light was murky, but I love this Scottish castle and I didn't have time to wait for the perfect light. By pushing 3200 ISO film to 6400, I made a picture that I feel works pretty well. The grainy texture is sympathetic with the rugged scenery and wintry weather.*

When choosing black-and-white film we have the complication of too much choice, mainly between the traditional and the chromogenic chemistry. As with slide and colour print film, the basic black-and-white workhorse is the 400 ISO. It's extremely versatile, the grain structure is smooth, and it can be pushed by 2 stops, if necessary, without the quality suffering too much. Also, it can reproduce a very large range of tones.

Specialist films

I KNOW THIS CHAPTER'S BEEN A BIT TECHNICAL *if you're new to photography, but that's all of the main film types covered now. I'm just going to take a couple of pages to tell you about two quite different types of film that just wouldn't fit anywhere else.*

Polaroid

Polaroid® instant photography has never really caught on with the public, probably because it's expensive and you can't easily make cheap prints from the original. But Polaroid is a much relied-upon tool of the professional. Most advertising and studio photographers take Polaroids as a test of their lighting and exposure before making the final shoot on conventional film.

POLAROID PICTURES

Polaroid is popular with art photographers too, who manipulate the processing to produce some extraordinary effects. You can also buy Polaroid transparency films. These are very interesting and worth experimenting with.

To process instant Polaroid transparencies you need a processing machine. It's small and inexpensive.

Polaroid makes a black-and-white print film that has a permanent negative from which you can make a print in the conventional way as well as getting an instant print. I like the tonal range of the 100 ISO black-and-white Polaroid slide film very much. The 400 ISO is good too, but very contrasty. The colour transparencies have a very unusual, almost painterly, quality. The emulsion is very fragile, however, and you need to mount the transparencies in glass slides or protective sheets as soon as possible to avoid scratches.

I have often used Polaroid black-and-white transparency film when giving lectures. I do a series of demonstration portraits and project them up on a huge screen.

Trivia...

Polaroid has a giant camera that you can hire, but you must hire the studio and assistant as well. It shoots a mind-blowing 50 x 60-cm (20 x 24-inch) picture.

Infrared film

Infrared film uses the invisible light at the infrared end of the spectrum. The film is sensitive to reflected light – the light bouncing off leaves, for example. The ISO ratings are only to be used as a guide, and the results, although unpredictable, can be spectacular: blue skies come out black and green foliage goes a ghostly white. I recommend you use a deep red filter with infrared film.

Infrared black-and-white film is very useful for cutting through haze, giving detail to infinity when very little is visible to the eye. Colour infrared was trendy in the late 60s and early 70s. The wild colours it reproduces – greenish faces, magenta grass – fitted in with the psychedelic scene at the time. If you decide to experiment with infrared – and why not? – you'll need to use a professional lab. And you must be very careful to load and unload the film in the dark.

A simple summary

✓ Brand name is not desperately important when buying film.

✓ There are three main types of film: colour negative, colour positive, and black-and-white.

✓ The term film speed refers to a film's sensitivity to light: the faster the film, the more sensitive it is to light.

✓ Film speed is shown in ISO ratings. The higher the ISO number, the faster the film.

✓ A 200 ISO film is twice as sensitive to light – it needs half as much light – as a 100 ISO film.

✓ Your standard film purchase for everyday use should be 400 ISO.

✓ The ISO setting on your camera should match the film inside it.

✓ Pushing a film means to expose it to less light than dictated by the ISO rating; it will increase the grain size on the print.

✓ Most professionals use colour slide film rather than print film. This gives them more creative control over the final image.

✓ It's worth experimenting with some of the chromogenic black-and-white films now available.

PART TWO

Chapter 5
What You Get for Your Money

Chapter 6
Things You Need to Know

Chapter 7
Flash

Chapter 8
Framing

Chapter 9
Troubleshooting

BIGGER ISN'T NECESSARILY BETTER

THE POINT-AND-SHOOT

PEOPLE OFTEN ASK MY ADVICE, starting with, "I only have a point-and-shoot camera but…". You should never apologize for your compact camera. Compacts are serious cameras, far *more sophisticated* than those used to shoot many of our favourite images from the past.

However, contrary to what the advertisements tell you, they can't take beautiful pictures by themselves. We take the pictures – cameras are *just machines* with no taste, no design sense, and no colour sense: that's where we come in, folks; that stuff is all down to us. In this section we'll look at the different types of point-and-shoot available and how to control all that *automation*. I want you to be able to make the camera do what you want it to do rather than what it has been programmed to do. So if you care how your pictures turn out, read on….

Chapter 5

What You Get for Your Money

THE TECHNOLOGY built into our point-and-shoot cameras has galloped ahead in recent years. These days, compacts employ weeny little electronic motors to automatically focus and zoom the lens, to turn on and complete the exposure on the flash, and to perform a seemingly infinite number of other functions – all the tasks that, until fairly recently, photographers had to work out for themselves. In this chapter we're going to look at the different types of compact that are on the market, and I'll discuss the advantages and disadvantages of each.

In this chapter...

✔ What are my options?

✔ Compact camera types

✔ What will I get for my outlay?

EVEN AN INEXPENSIVE CAMERA CAN PRODUCE EXCELLENT RESULTS WITH A LITTLE CREATIVE PLANNING

What are my options?

IN CHAPTER 3, *we looked at the choices available to you when buying a new camera. In this chapter we're going to concentrate on the different types of compact camera in more detail. For those of you who are planning to buy a new point-and-shoot – whether it's your first or an upgrade – it's important to know what you get for your money.*

You may be asking yourself, "Is it worth jumping from the £50 price point to £300?", for example. Well, there's no easy answer, but I'll try to simplify things by putting point-and-shoot cameras into four major categories:

 35mm compacts

 APS, or Advanced Photo System, cameras

 Digital point-and-shoots

 Single-use cameras

APS CAMERAS

Further to this you need to know that, in general, you get what you pay for. In short, the more money you spend, the more modes and facilities you get:

1 Your flash power will increase

2 Your zoom lens will zoom further

3 You'll have greater control over exposures

4 Your lens will be better quality

 There are new point-and-shoots coming on to the market almost daily. Keep up to date by reading reviews in photography magazines.

FUJIFILM
nexia
4100 ix Z
MRC

COMPACT CAMERA WITH ZOOM LENS

Unique selling points

Camera manufacturers, like all electronics companies, build in loads of "unique selling points" (USPs, sometimes just called SPs) that they want us to believe we can't do without. Of course, these USPs are meant to seduce us into parting with as much money as possible. I want to help you make decisions that result in you owning the camera that suits your requirements and your pocket, not the camera that the industry wants to sell you.

Don't pay for stuff you don't want – check the camera specifications carefully.

Compact camera types

AS I MENTIONED, *there are four basic types of compact camera and you may be interested in any one or more of them. For example, although you own (or will own) a 35mm compact, you might still buy some single-use waterproof cameras for when you go to the beach. Let's have a look at the cameras.*

35mm compacts

The 35mm point-and-shoot has been around a long time: the very first one was marketed in 1976 by Konica. It's based on the 35mm rangefinder and SLR (single lens reflex) cameras that have been the workhorse of the professional photojournalist since Leica came on the scene in 1925. The film for these cameras comes in metal cassettes and the camera shoots 36 x 24-mm (1½ x 1-inch) negatives or transparencies (slides). The 35mm point-and-shoot is still preferred by the serious photographer over the APS camera because it produces a larger negative. This, in turn, means prints of a higher quality, because an APS negative requires more enlargement to produce a print of the same size. The 35mm compact also wins when compared to the digital compact – the image quality is superior – but digital technology is closing the gap rapidly.

35MM COMPACT CAMERA

APS cameras

When the first APS camera was launched, I was very dismissive of it as simply a marketing scam. After all, the negative size is about half that of a 35mm negative so the *quality* can't be that good. And although APS cameras are more compact, they are not so much smaller as to make a great deal of difference in your pocket or handbag.

DEFINITION

Photographers use the word **quality** *as an all-embracing term that covers sharpness, grain size, colour saturation, and contrast.*

However, what has made the APS an attractive alternative to 35mm is the choice of print formats. You can choose from three different print shapes at the flick of a switch on the camera, and you can keep changing throughout the film. When you get your film developed, you are automatically supplied with an index print of all the pictures on the film in miniature, with each picture numbered, making it easy to pick the image you want to blow up. Although you'll notice that the quality of a large print (over 10 x 8 inches [25 x 20 cm]) is inferior to one made from a 35mm negative, the quality is okay, and the convenience factor considerable.

I think the APS is the ideal camera to record your lifestyle, to use as a sort of visual diary.

APS CAMERA

The designs are getting pretty sexy too, ensuring that you will look super-cool when wearing one around your neck! The whole design concept of APS was to make picture-taking foolproof – and they've got pretty close.

■ **APS cameras** *offer the user three different print formats: classic or C-prints (shown here by a black outline), high-vision or H-prints (yellow outline), and panoramic or P-prints (red outline). All of these are obtained from the standard APS negative. You specify your chosen format on the camera before each shot, and your photo developer prints the image to your choice.*

Digital point-and-shoots

The newest addition to the point-and-shoot world of photography is the digital camera. Photography without film is the greatest technical advancement in the last 100 years. The actual taking of the pictures is the same as with a conventional film camera, but the image is recorded on a light-sensing chip instead of on light-sensitive film. The camera's computer stores the images digitally and you can then download those digital files into your computer. If you have the appropriate software you can retouch them, manipulate them, print them out, or e-mail them to friends and family, who can view them on their monitor or print them out themselves. It's amazing really.

■ **You may be unfamiliar** *with the shapes and layouts of some digital cameras, but don't let that put you off. All the usual controls are there, and within a short amount of time you will be comfortable with them all and snapping away just as confidently as with any compact camera.*

Everything that I say about taking pictures throughout this book applies as much to digital photography as it does to shooting on film. (I've also devoted the last two chapters of the book to digital work.)

The great advantage of digital photography is that you can make your own prints, which means no more developing and printing costs.

■ **In bright light** *the LCD screen may be difficult to view, so some cameras offer a brightness control to help compensate for such conditions.*

Digital disadvantages

The main disadvantage of going digital is that the cameras and equipment are still more expensive than their conventional counterparts. And, unless you are spending several thousand pounds, the quality of digital blow-ups is still inferior to that of blow-ups made from film. Digital prices are coming down fast, though, and within a few years will be competitive with conventional cameras. Another big problem for me is the time gap between pictures: while the camera is storing the image you can't take another picture. This takes several seconds, which I find frustrating.

Although most of the new digital models look much like a conventional camera, the big difference is that digital cameras have an *LCD* viewing screen, which you can use as a viewfinder, as well as providing an optical viewfinder.

> **DEFINITION**
>
> LCD *stands for liquid crystal display.*

Don't use your LCD as your sole viewfinder.

To avoid draining your battery, you should use the LCD for playback only; have a look at the picture you've just taken and store it if it's to your liking, or erase it and reshoot if you're dissatisfied with it.

Single-use cameras

Most film manufacturers market disposable single-use cameras that come loaded with film, usually 400 ISO. These cameras have a fixed-focal-length lens, one shutter speed (usually $\frac{1}{1000}$ of a second), and a built-in flash that works efficiently up to 4 metres (13 ft). In bright light these machines produce surprisingly good results. There are also underwater versions available.

■ **Don't risk ruining** *your expensive compact with sand and seawater – just buy a single-use waterproof camera for beach holidays.*

Single-use cameras are useful if you forget your camera, or for taking to the beach to avoid ruining your normal compact.

I think the underwater ones are great fun to take on holidays as an extra, especially if you anticipate doing some scuba diving or snorkelling.

Special compacts

There are some other compacts that don't quite fit into the four basic types that I've laid out above. These include the underwater and sport cameras.

Underwater compacts

There are several weatherproof compacts on the market with underwater capabilities. They're waterproof, sandproof, and dustproof, and they can take underwater pictures down to a depth of about 5 metres (16 ft). You can drop them on the beach and wash them off later without worrying about ruining them. They perform very well above water too.

Sport, or off-road, cameras

These cameras are resistant to water, sand, and dust, and are useful for outdoor enthusiasts. However, sport cameras are not suitable for underwater photography.

■ **Waterproof and stylish** – *what more could you ask for on the beach?*

What will I get for my outlay?

SO LET'S HAVE A LOOK NOW *at roughly what you might expect to get for your money. I have broken the market down into five price points. As time moves on, we find that we get more features on our electrical goods for less money, but then you have to consider inflation too.... So use this guide as a pointer, not as the last word on the subject.*

Level 1 (under £40)

The basic 35mm point-and-shoot camera will have a fixed-focal-length lens that has no autofocus. The manufacturers set the focus on the lens at about 2–2½ metres (6–8 ft). The fixed aperture, between f5.6 and f8 on a lens of around 32–36mm, will hold most pictures sharp. (These specifications will vary between cameras.) The shutter will be fixed at about ¹⁄₁₂₅ of a second.

BASIC POINT-AND-SHOOT

> **DEFINITION**
>
> The term **flash throw** is used to mean the distance from the camera that the flash will illuminate adequately for a photograph.

Finally, you will have a flash, probably with an on/off switch; **flash throw** will be approximately 6 metres (20 ft) when using 400 ISO film. In spite of their limitations, you can take some lovely pictures with these snappers if your eye is good enough.

Level 2 (£40–£120)

At this slightly higher price level, cameras include a zoom lens with autofocus. You will also get a more powerful flash and a speed shutter that varies between about ¹⁄₁₅ and ¹⁄₂₅₀ of a second. Another benefit of paying slightly more is that your viewfinder will be more accurate.

POINT-AND-SHOOT WITH ZOOM LENS

Level 3 (£120–£300)

This medium-cost range is a mind-boggling place to be. You just get a bit more of everything. But most important is the general improvement in lens quality – the image is so much sharper! There are some great-value cameras in this range if you carefully match your requirements with the mode facilities available. At this price you can start to take control of exposure since some models include exposure compensation and back-light compensation.

Level 4 (£300–£1,000)

Once again, in this price bracket you get more of everything and a general all-round improvement in quality on all of the functions. But when you get into spending this sort of serious money, most of it goes on lens quality and flash power. Watch out for the old USP gimmicks – just buy what you need.

Level 5 (big bucks!)

These so-called super-compacts can cost thousands of pounds and are targeted at the professional as a "pocket-sized snapshot camera". Ironically they usually come with a fixed-focal-length lens, although it is admittedly of very high quality with large apertures (f2 and f2.8). Compacts in this price bracket have manual overrides on all of the automatic modes. Aperture and shutter speed are indicated and can even be manually operated.

A simple summary

✓ When considering buying a compact camera there are four major categories from which you'll have to choose.

✓ Compact cameras can vary in cost from small two-figure sums right up to four figures.

✓ Generally speaking, you get what you pay for.

✓ The 35mm compacts are capable of producing better-quality images than APS and digital cameras.

✓ Digital cameras are more expensive but they don't use film; this saves you developing and printing costs.

✓ Super-compacts are aimed at very experienced photographers.

Chapter 6

Things You Need to Know

I'VE INCLUDED THIS CHAPTER because I think it's important that we get the point-and-shoot basics out of the way. You may feel that some of the information here is too basic, stuff you already know, but I think it's useful for information to be reiterated. Even if some of this chapter is not crucial to you being able to shoot good pictures, you should get your head around it so you know exactly what that computer and those electric motors are doing inside your camera when you push the button.

In this chapter...

✓ Holding the camera

✓ Exposure – what the camera is doing

✓ Autofocus

✓ Loads of modes

Holding the camera

I'M GOING TO START THIS CHAPTER in perhaps the most obvious place – obvious because the great majority of the time you will be holding your camera when you take a picture. It is therefore very important that you know how to hold your camera correctly. And yet, so many people hold their cameras incorrectly, if not all the time then certainly some of the time.

CORRECT HANDLING

There are two vital points to remember when holding your camera:

1. Hold your camera absolutely still when taking a shot. Most out-of-focus prints are caused by camera shake. This can be avoided if you gently squeeze the shutter release button rather than pressing down hard.

If you wish to take still-life photographs or other shots that would require slow shutter speeds then you should consider buying a tripod.

2. Keep your fingers away from the flash, the lens, and the viewfinder as well as the small autofocus, self-timer, and autoexposure windows. If you cover any of these you will prevent them from functioning properly and, in the case of the lens, you will end up with a picture of your finger.

■ **The camera** is well supported and the fingers are clear of the flash, autofocus windows, and lens. If you are using the telephoto setting, support the extended zoom lens with your forefinger.

■ **Here, the fingers** of the left hand are obstructing both the flash and autofocus windows. Also, the fingers of both hands are far too close to the lens.

Exposure – what the camera is doing

FORTUNATELY, ON A COMPACT CAMERA, both the aperture and shutter speed are controlled automatically. However, an understanding of how they work will enable you to assess what your camera is doing in different lighting conditions and will empower you to manipulate and control the automatic functions if you wish. (For more detailed information on exposure have another look at Chapter 2.)

A point-and-shoot camera automatically sets the aperture and shutter speed to give the correct exposure for the light conditions and type of film you are using.

This automation, combined with the versatility of colour print films, means that you will nearly always be able to get a print from your negative. Occasionally, however, there are certain situations in which the automatic exposure may be fooled into giving the wrong reading. If you wish to photograph a relatively small, dark figure against a large area of white, for example, the automatic exposure will correctly expose for the background but, in doing so, underexpose for the figure. The reverse is also true – when photographing a small, light figure against a large, dark background the figure will be overexposed and the background correctly exposed.

Outsmarting autoexposure

On some of the mid-price compacts, there are several ways of overcoming this problem that you get with autoexposure.

 You may have a back-light button on your camera, which is the equivalent of opening the aperture another 1½ f-stops.

 If your compact has an exposure-compensation mode, you can use that.

Some point-and-shoots have a spot-focus, or focus-lock, mode that the camera uses to read the exposure off a small area, marked by a spot or square in the viewfinder. Place the spot over the subject, push lightly on the shutter release button to lock the focus (and exposure), then, still holding the button down, recompose and shoot.

If your camera offers you none of these modes, you may be able to use one of your built-in flash modes (see Chapter 7 for more details about the flash).

Another problem you might encounter is if you are trying to take a portrait in the shade with a brightly lit area in the background. If your compact is set to its fully automatic mode, the flash will probably go off to throw more light on the subject being photographed. However, if you do not want flash, turn it off and use the exposure compensation, back-light button, or spot-focus mode to solve the problem.

DEFINITION

The word **pan** *is a verb meaning to move the camera in the same direction as a moving subject, always keeping the subject in approximately the same position within the frame. Panning is also used in TV and the movies to follow the on-screen action, and in music to move sound from one speaker to another.*

Shutter speeds

Another thing about point-and-shoot cameras is that their shutter speeds are not very fast. Most compact cameras have a maximum shutter speed of between $\frac{1}{250}$ and $\frac{1}{360}$ of a second, so if you wish to freeze fast-moving subjects you need to **pan** the camera with your subject. This will blur the background but give you a frozen subject.

Autofocus

NEARLY ALL COMPACT CAMERAS focus automatically. But you have to make sure you know how to use this system correctly. I found the compact autofocus system difficult at first. I was used to the SLR viewfinder in which the image goes in and out of focus as you move the lens, whereas everything in the viewfinder of a compact always looks sharp.

When you look through the viewfinder of all but the very cheapest compact cameras, you will notice a pair of square brackets in the centre – these are focusing brackets. In order to get a correctly focused picture you must ensure your subject falls within the area marked out by the brackets. However, the central positioning of the focusing brackets can lead you into the trap of taking pictures in which the main subject is always in the centre of the frame. You don't have to do that!

USING FOCUSING BRACKETS

USING FOCUS LOCK

If you want to take a shot in which your
main subject is off centre, you can use the
focus-lock, or pre-focus, system.

1 Centre the subject

*Compose your picture with the subject inside the
brackets. (Note that if you are taking a close-up shot,
ensure your subject falls within the close-up autofocus
brackets. See your camera's instruction manual.)*

2 Lock the focus

*Press the shutter-release button slightly (about halfway)
and keep it held down. This locks the focus on.*

3 Reposition your subject

Recompose the picture with the subject off centre.

Don't change your distance from the subject when you recompose —
the focus has been set at the original distance.

4 Take the picture!

*Press the shutter-release button the rest of the
way down.*

Do use the focus-lock technique. It's very useful and enables you to make more
interesting compositions.

Most of the autofocus systems on compacts work using an infrared
light signal which bounces off the subject and returns to the
camera. The distance is measured by the autofocus sensor, and
the lens elements adjust in order to focus accurately on the subject.

Infinity focusing

Another useful function to have is an infinity setting. This not only allows you to take sharp pictures of faraway objects such as distant mountains, but also allows you to take photographs through glass – for example, through a car or train window – without interfering with the autofocus mechanism.

To prevent unwanted reflections when photographing through a window, position yourself as close to the glass as you can and drape a coat or rug over both your head and the camera.

If you want to photograph a stationary object from a moving vehicle, focus on a point ahead or behind the object to reduce the movement and, therefore, the chance of blur on the picture.

Loads of modes

SOME OF THE MODERN *compact cameras come packed with a huge amount of modes and programs, each of which is identified by a visual symbol that appears on a dial or in an LCD panel on the camera.*

LCD PANEL

I can never remember which functions each symbol equates to, or which button (or buttons) I need to push to recall a particular program, so I keep the symbols written down in my pocket for reference. You could also stick a list to the back of the camera.

Modes you might encounter

At this point I'd like to say that no matter how much information there is in this book, and how useful you might find it, this book is not a replacement for your camera's instruction manual. Each camera is different and I can't cover every quirk of every model in this guide.

Read your camera's instruction manual carefully and don't lose it.

Apart from such essentials as automatic exposure, focus, and flash there are many other gimmicky devices available. Some of them might be on your current camera or on the next one you decide to buy.

Here is a list of some of the most common facilities you might find on your camera. Some of these may sound like just the thing you need, and you may hate the idea of others.

- **Mid-roll review with memory** This is useful if you want to take a few shots on ultrafast film, for example, and then go back to your normal film. By pressing a button the film rewinds and takes note of how many exposures were used. When that film is replaced, the camera winds it on to the correct position.
- **Self timer** This function allows you about 10 seconds to get into the picture before the shutter fires.
- **Remote control** Fires the shutter from up to about 5 metres (16 ft) away.
- **Multiple-exposure mode** Using this mode you can shoot two or more exposures on the same negative for special-effects photography.
- **Continuous-shooting mode** Keeps taking pictures for as long as you keep the shutter button pressed down, up to two shots per second.
- **Interval exposure** Sets the camera to fire automatically at intervals without anyone being present.
- **TV mode** Enables you to take pictures off a TV screen.
- **Timecode mode** Automatically prints the date and time on the picture so you'll always know when it was taken.
- **Print-a-message mode** Allows you to print "Happy Birthday" or some such message on to your pictures.

Remember, don't buy facilities you don't want – they cost money and make the camera too complicated.

A simple summary

✓ The camera should be held absolutely still when taking a picture.

✓ You should ensure the flash, lens, viewfinder, and other essential windows are not obstructed by fingers.

✓ Compact cameras set the aperture and shutter speeds for you.

✓ Most compacts have some sort of autoexposure override built in.

✓ To get the best out of your autofocus system you should use the focus-lock technique.

✓ There is a huge array of modes available on compact cameras these days. Buy only what you need and learn how they work.

Chapter 7

Flash

FLASH IS A WONDERFUL LIGHT SOURCE that can be used to capture a picture that otherwise would not be possible. But do we use it too often? And do we use it creatively enough? This chapter will help you sort out one flash mode from the other and help you to use each of them in more imaginative ways.

In this chapter...
- ✓ *How far will the flash reach?*
- ✓ *Flash modes*
- ✓ *Thinking about ambient light*
- ✓ *Party time*
- ✓ *Flash tricks*

OKAY, SO YOUR FLASH MAY NOT LIGHT UP THE SKIES LIKE THIS ONE...

How far will the flash reach?

EVERY COMPACT CAMERA has a built-in flash, the power of which (in other words, the effective distance at which it can correctly expose the film) varies between cameras. You should check this before you purchase your model.

I am constantly amazed at the time and film (and therefore money) that is wasted by people using compact cameras with the flash turned on for long-distance shots. An example of the sort of thing I mean is all of the little flashes going off around the stadium at a televised night-time football match. At those sorts of distance the flash will have no chance of making an exposure.

FLASH DISTANCES

Take note of this guide to flash distances – it could save you money. Three variables to be aware of are the power of the flash, the speed of the film, and the difference of efficiency between the wide-angle and telephoto settings on your zoom. Once you understand these principles you will achieve more successful flash photography.

Approximate distance reached by flash – metres (feet)

	40 (132)	3200 ISO
	35 (115)	
	30 (98)	
	25 (82)	
	20 (65)	
	15 (49)	
	10 (33)	
	5 (16)	
	0	

| | Wide-angle | Telephoto | | Wide-angle | Telephoto | | Wide-angle | Telephoto |
| LOW-COST CAMERAS | | | MEDIUM-COST CAMERAS | | | HIGH-COST CAMERAS | | |

If you want to take long-distance night-time shots, use fast film (1000–3200 ISO) and turn off the flash. The shutter speed will be slow, so you must support the camera by leaning against a post or seat, but it's worth trying since you can get some very atmospheric shots.

This is also a good way of taking pictures at concerts or plays where flash photography is forbidden. If you can't switch off your camera's flash, hold your finger over it or cover it with some (removable) opaque tape instead. This is just as effective.

Flash modes

IF YOUR COMPACT CAMERA HAS A FLASH, and all but the very cheapest do, you will probably be able to exercise some degree of control over when the flash is activated. That way you can decide, for example, not to use it at all if you're taking a bright daytime shot. Let's have a look at some of the modes that are most commonly found on point-and-shoots.

Auto flash mode

When set on automatic, or auto, the flash fires automatically if the camera assesses that there's not enough light to expose the film correctly. This means that your flash may go off not just at night or indoors but also if you are trying to take a picture in dark shadow, for instance.

Flash off mode

This is a very useful mode. If you are in a situation where you you think the camera would fire the flash if set to auto, and that is not what you want, then you can simply switch the flash off. Remember, though, that the shutter speed may then be slower, so make sure you can hold the camera steady, preferably using some sort of support.

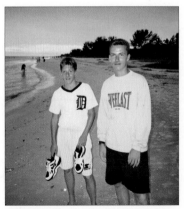

■ **The auto flash** *has done a great job here of filling in the faces that would have otherwise been in shadow from the fading twilight sun.*

Anytime flash mode

With this mode, you can use the flash anytime you like – for example, if you feel the subject needs extra light to "fill in" an area that might otherwise be in shadow. The camera balances daylight and flash to ensure correct exposure. This mode is different to auto flash since you have to make a creative decision to use it. Auto flash will often fill in areas of shadow, but it may do so when you don't want it to.

Auto flash with sync mode, or night flash

If you are taking a portrait of a group of people at night against a background of city lights, the flash will normally give the correct exposure for the figures, meaning that the background will be underexposed. The slow sync mode gives a longer exposure for the background while exposing correctly for the flash to produce a fully balanced photograph. When in this mode, the camera will select a relatively slow shutter speed (about ¼ of a second), so you will have to lean against a sturdy object to prevent camera shake.

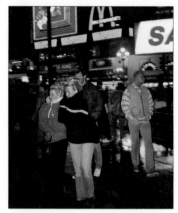

■ **The camera's night flash mode** *has worked out the shutter speed needed to expose the film for the lights of London's Piccadilly Circus and also how much flash is required to light the people.*

Red-eye reduction mode

Everybody has examples of pictures taken with a flash in which the subject appears to have bright red eyes. It's caused when light conditions are poor and the pupils of the eyes enlarge to allow more light to enter the eye so that we can see better. As a result, when the flash goes off, the light is reflected off the red blood vessels behind the pupil back into the camera giving the subject the dreaded red eye! The red-eye reduction mode aims to reduce this effect by firing off several small flashes to make the pupils of the eyes contract before the picture is taken with the full-power flash. But, in my opinion, it doesn't work. Furthermore, the delay between pushing the button and the shutter firing on red-eye mode is too long and facial expressions you wanted to capture are gone by the time the shot is taken.

Shoot without the red-eye reduction mode and use a red-eye retouch pen on the prints. It's easy to do and works a treat!

Thinking about ambient light

REMEMBER THAT, UNLESS YOU TELL the camera otherwise, most point-and-shoots will automatically fire the flash when they calculate that the light is too low or that the subject is back-lit, in the shadows, or in front of a brightly lit background.

You need to be constantly on your guard about this. You need to ask yourself, "Do I want flash for this picture?" You may want your foreground figures to be in silhouette, therefore you don't want flash (it would fill in and destroy the silhouette).

■ **Comparison pieces:** *The first picture here was shot without flash and the film has been exposed for the background, leaving the lady in the foreground as a silhouette. For the second shot, I turned on the flash and created a good balance between the lady, her house, and her butler. This is the sort of difference the anytime flash mode can make.*

You may want to use a slow shutter speed and support the camera on a tripod, table, or some other stable surface. In such cases, you must also turn off the flash. You may want a slow shutter speed in order to deliberately blur movement, or you may want to induce camera movement in order to create a blurred effect on the whole picture. In either of these cases, again, you will need to turn off the flash. Make sure that it's you who is making the flash decisions and not the camera.

Cameras have no artistic taste. The creative alternative to flash is a slow shutter speed and a tripod (a light one that will fit in your case). If you're interested in low-light subjects you will need a tripod anyway.

Party time

MANY YOUNGSTERS *of school and college age shoot a high proportion of their film photographing their friends at parties and other social occasions. These pictures provide great pleasure at the time and will be wonderful memories and reminders of their youthful high jinks. The pictures will be a record of their "good ol' days".*

■ **This typical party picture** – *the sort of thing memories are made of* – *was shot using 800 ISO film to preserve some of the ambient lighting.*

In such cases it is likely that a great many of these pictures will be taken with a point-and-shoot with the flash on, so I thought it appropriate to pass on a few party flash tips.

a Use fast film (800–1600 ISO). This is because fast film requires less light to make an exposure, therefore it needs less flash, which, in turn, means the battery will last longer and the flash will recycle faster. Also, the fast film will gather some of the room's ambient light, so you will get more of the location's atmosphere.

b Try to use the wide-angle setting on your camera rather than the telephoto setting. The wide-angle lets in three to four times as much light as the tele end of the zoom lens, so here again you will use less flash.

c Take a spare battery in your pocket or handbag in case the flash starts to take too long to warm up.

If you're going to a place or area where you fear your camera might get broken or stolen, take a single-use camera instead.

Flash tricks

HERE'S A COUPLE of nice creative things you can do with a compact flash. I'm sure you can come up with some others; just get out there and start flashing!

Portrait flash

One of the problems with point-and-shoot flash is that it's such a harsh light source for portraits. However, by placing a piece of tissue or tracing paper over the flash and using fast film, which is inherently softer than slow film, you can produce a more flattering portrait. Especially outside in the daylight, where the flash diffuses even more.

Flash and the wind

Point-and-shoot cameras cope very well with photographing flowers and plants. One of the great problems when shooting in gardens is the sort of movement of your subject that is caused by even the slightest of breezes. The flash freezes the movement and produces a beautiful, sharp picture.

Be careful when taking close-ups of flowers – be sure that you are framing inside the close-up markings in the viewfinder.

If it's a very sunny day, try to shoot in the shade, or shade off the flower, to prevent a double image, that is, a daylight exposure and a flash exposure on one photograph.

A simple summary

✔ Your flash will only be of any use for short distances. If you are going to take long-distance, low-light shots, use fast film, turn off the flash, and use a good support.

✔ You don't always have to have your flash on. Try out all of your camera's flash modes.

✔ The creative decision to use the flash should be yours. Don't set your flash mode to auto – choose when you wish to use it.

✔ Don't rely solely on flash for capturing a party atmosphere. Combine it with fast film and a wide-angle lens setting.

Chapter 8

Framing

THIS CHAPTER IS CALLED FRAMING to distinguish it from the later chapter on composition. By framing, I mean the ways in which you can improve your pictures by learning to really look through that viewfinder and see the glaring problems that prevent them from looking great. I think of composition as the next stage on from framing – the arty, creative version. This chapter is devoted to practical composition, if you like, and I'll give you some tips about using your camera's facilities and your eye to turn your snapshots into attractive pictures by framing them well.

In this chapter...

✓ *Searching out the ugly*

✓ *Filling the frame*

✓ *Composing with the zoom*

✓ *Horizontal, vertical, or panoramic?*

✓ *Camera angles – the highs and lows*

GATEWAYS AND ARCHWAYS CAN BE USED TO CREATE A FRAME WITHIN A FRAME

Searching out the ugly

I'M SURE WE ALL START OUT by trying to search out the beautiful things in our surroundings and in our photographs. Surely that's what photography is all about, isn't it? Well... yes and no.

The first step you need to take in order to end up with a beautiful picture in your viewfinder is to be aware of the ugly things, those things that destroy so many rookies' pictures.

It's so often a pole that appears to be growing out of your son's head that destroys a potentially lovely holiday portrait, or the empty beer cans that can spoil a landscape.

Only the beautiful remains

Good framing and composition are very much about searching out the ugly in order to remove it. And once you've removed the ugly, you'll have a good chance of finding that you are left with just the beautiful.

Many professional photographers who are digitally inclined remove rubbish and reframe their compositions later in Photoshop®. I'm old-fashioned – I like to get it right in the camera!

■ **The lamppost growing** out of the top of the girl's head in the first shot here is a classic framing mistake that we've all made! Really look through the viewfinder at every part of the picture, not just the main subject. By simply moving a little you can prevent this sort of thing from happening.

Filling the frame

EARLY ON IN OUR PHOTOGRAPHIC JOURNEY, most of us expect objects in the viewfinder to look much bigger on the final picture than they really are. You may have been surprised and disappointed in the past to discover that, say, your daughter had only taken up a small proportion of the print.

DEFINITION

The word **frame** is used to describe the area of the world that you see through your camera's viewfinder.

So let's get bold. Look at all the space that is surrounding your subject and go much closer. In fact, fill the *frame* with the subject matter.

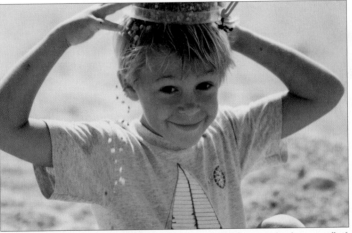

■ **Make an effort** to get in close and take big, bold pictures. It will feel unnatural at first, especially if you are used to shooting people small in the frame, but the results will be so much better.

When you get used to filling the frame, you can then start backing off occasionally and making more artistic compositions. But first of all – get in there, be bold, move closer!

Remember that, at the end of the day, composition is subjective. As long as the result is how you saw it, it's okay.

Townley Grammar School for Girls

■ **For this picture,**
*I wanted to emphasize
the action rather than
the balloon, which is
why I have framed the
shot this way. I used
my compact camera's
zoom on its longest
telephoto setting –
105mm – and left just
enough of the balloon
for it to be identifiable.
The zoom was essential
since I was not able to
move any closer.*

Composing with the zoom

ALTHOUGH I TALK ABOUT LENSING SEPARATELY later on in the book, I think it's important that I make specific mention here for point-and-shoot users. The telephoto end of your zoom lens does, of course, take you closer to your subject, and your wide-angle end allows you to get more of the subject into the frame, but the zoom does more than that.

Perspective control

The zoom lens is your tool for controlling perspective. You can change the relationship between the foreground and background by changing the focal length of the lens – that is, by zooming in. I can best demonstrate this point through the use of a couple of images.

■ **Changing perspective:** *The top picture was shot with the zoom set at 32mm (wide-angle) and the bottom shot was taken at 85mm (telephoto). Note the different size of the building in relation to the woman in the two images. This is an example of using your compact camera's zoom as a creative tool to manipulate perspective.*

Your zoom lens is not an alternative to walking closer to the subject. Sometimes the wide-angle lens used close to the subject gives a better composition with greater perspective than the same picture zoomed in on a telephoto setting.

Horizontal, vertical, or panoramic?

JUST THROUGH THE DESIGN of the camera and the dimensions of the pictures that APS and 35mm cameras produce, we are presented with a very important compositional decision every time we pick one up: "Will I shoot this picture horizontally or vertically?"

Most amateurs naturally shoot horizontally because that is the way the camera takes them when you simply pick it up and snap. It's not for me to say or advise you on which subjects should be vertical and which should be horizontal – that's your decision. But, please, please, make a decision.

Don't just shoot with your creative brain in neutral. Which shape will make the subject look most interesting? Or "different"? Or dynamic?

■ **It seems so obvious,** *but deciding whether to shoot horizontal, vertical, or panoramic is a major compositional choice. So often we just snap away without thinking, but by turning the camera in our hand we can make a completely different picture. Compare these two shots taken in Venice.*

Now, of course, to add to your list of options, many of the latest point-and-shoot cameras have a panoramic mode as well. This can look really good – in fact, you can create some wild-looking vertical panoramas!

The more subjects you shoot in each of the dimensions available to you, the more you will learn about basic format composition.

INTERNET

www.apogeephoto.com/ PFYP.shtml

This page of Apogee Photo's web site is called "Photography for Young People", but it's also great for beginners. The topics covered change from time to time, but do take a look.

■ **The extreme proportions** of the *panoramic format can produce some unusual compositions. Play with it and see what you think of the results!*

Camera angles – the highs and lows

THE LAST PIECE OF SEEMINGLY OBVIOUS ADVICE *I'm going to pass on to you in this chapter – and this is something that I still have to remind myself of – is that your standing position is not the only camera angle available to you.*

The easiest thing you can do to alter the look of a photograph is move. Whether it's a jump to the left or a step to the right. Whether you climb a ladder or lie flat on your stomach. Whatever. The worst thing you can do is take all your pictures from the same eye-level position. Move around.

■ **Here's an example** *of the sort of beach snap you've probably seen a million times – family members and holidaymakers all around their umbrellas, which take centre stage....*

■ **... But couldn't it have been** *more adventurous? If the umbrellas are going to be so prominent, get right in there and take a picture of the umbrellas! This unusual angle makes for a more interesting photograph.*

■ **By kneeling down,** *I shot this picture from the little girl's height, making Mum look huge. Make your compositions stronger by varying your eye level.*

Change your point of view

Make an effort to look at things from a different perspective. No doubt this is a metaphor for our lives in general!

I'll repeat this tip several times throughout the book because it's so easy to do and yet it can make such a dramatic improvement to the impact of your photographs.

When a subject is looking a bit on the boring side, try standing on a chair and looking down on it. Or sit on the ground and look up at it.

A simple summary

✓ There's more to good photography than just focusing on the most beautiful things around you. To take a good photograph, you need to "edit out" the worst parts of your surroundings too.

✓ Your subject will only fill the frame on your prints if they first fill the frame in your viewfinder. Get closer to your subject and fill the frame!

✓ You can control perspective through use of your zoom lens. That means that you can change the visual relationship between your subject and the background.

✓ Your zoom lens is not an alternative to walking closer to your subject. The more you experiment with the different effects you can achieve, the more you will understand when and when not to use your zoom.

✓ There is more than one way to hold a camera and you should make a choice for each and every picture you take.

✓ There is more than one viewpoint from which you can take any picture. Move around, up, and down in search of the best shot.

Chapter 9

Troubleshooting

SINCE THIS IS THE LAST DEDICATED point-and-shoot chapter, let's have a look at some of my compact catastrophes and see what went wrong. "Is this brave or foolhardy?" I ask myself. The answer is that, hopefully, by looking at these pictures and understanding why they look the way they do, you'll be in a better position to prevent the same things from happening to your would-be masterpieces. Go on, laugh it up!

In this chapter...
- ✓ *Problem pictures*
- ✓ *Framing foul-ups*
- ✓ *Fudged focusing*
- ✓ *Exposure accidents*
- ✓ *Obstructions*
- ✓ *Lab problems*

IDENTIFYING AND SOLVING YOUR PROBLEMS COULD LEAD THE WAY TO A MASTERPIECE

Problem pictures

AT ONE TIME OR ANOTHER I'm sure you've had some horrible prints back from the lab – I certainly have! And depending on which lab you use, you may have had some sort of professional analysis of what made them look so bad, probably a little removable sticker stuck to the offending photo.

Over the next few pages you'll see some of my bad prints – a sort of rogues' gallery – along with my explanation of how the problem could have been avoided. Some of the mishaps are the fault of the lab and some are mine. I trust that by publicly humiliating myself in this way I will help you to become a better photographer.

Framing foul-ups

PROBABLY ONE OF THE MOST fundamental difficulties people have with point-and-shoot cameras is that of framing. This may be because, unlike on an SLR, you do not see through the viewfinder what the camera "sees" in the lens.

If you look at the front of your compact you'll see what I mean: your viewfinder goes all the way through the camera and the lens is a separate bit altogether. But, of course, there are other reasons why your framing can go awry....

■ **Sloping horizons:** *If the horizon is sloping down from left to right it usually means you've stabbed down on the shutter and jerked the camera out of alignment. Remember to squeeze the shutter gently.*

■ **A slight cut-off** *usually means that you haven't allowed for the 15 per cent crop that the minilab machine takes off every picture. Ask the staff for a hand print.*

Fudged focusing

IT'S TRUE TO SAY *that a great many point-and-shoots have no focusing flexibility at all. So let's see how I could have avoided the problems below. (You may find it useful to have another look at Chapter 6, too.)*

■ **The reason** *why the focusing is a bit off here is a combination of two factors: I hadn't turned the flash on, and I had loaded too slow a film for the low-light conditions.*

■ **In this shot,** *I've got a bit of camera shake due to the light being insufficient and the flash having nothing to expose. It would have been fine if the camera had been supported somehow.*

■ **Take a step back:** *This is simply a case of being too close to the subject for the point-and-shoot to be able to focus correctly.*

■ **You can avoid the problem** *of the autofocus trying to focus on the car or bus window by setting it to infinity.*

Exposure accidents

IT'S ANNOYING when a beautiful portrait turns out to be covered in darkness; it wasn't even that dark when you shot it, was it? Or, at the other extreme, the whole image looks bleached out. What gives?

■ **Never open the back** of the camera until the film is finished and rewound, or this is what you'll get. It can happen by accident, so be careful.

■ **The flare effect** seen in this picture is due to shooting right into the direction of the sun. A few steps to the right might have made all the difference.

■ **The person** intended as the subject in this shot was too small in the frame for the flash to fire automatically. The flash should have been set to "anytime".

■ **The dreaded red eye:** Red-eye reduction modes don't work. Turn it off and use a retouch pen on the print or make amends on your computer using Photoshop®.

Flash exposure problems

As we've seen on the previous page, exposure problems are often the result of the camera not being able to deal with the ambient light conditions around it. But sometimes the problem is not surrounding light, but the light created by the flash.

■ **The right-hand side** *of the settee is too close to the flash and has bleached out. In such cases, move further back or recompose the shot so everything is the same distance from the camera.*

■ **The negative** *has been overexposed because I was too close with the flash. All is not lost though – if you get a picture looking like this ask your lab to reprint it for you.*

■ **Take care** *when you are shooting against a shiny surface such as a window or a mirror. You can overcome this glare by shooting at an angle.*

■ **The automatic processing machine** *couldn't cope with the huge exposure range on the negative. However, you should be able to get it right if you ask for a hand print.*

Obstructions

PERHAPS IT WOULDN'T be so bad if you could say, "Nice close-up of my fingertip", but the truth is that the obstruction, whatever it is, is never a nice close-up – it's just a big out-of-focus blur ruining your picture.

■ **These two pictures** have suffered from slight negligence on my part. The shot on the left has my camera strap across it – it's so easy to do – and, yes, that's my finger in front of the lens above. Hold that camera correctly!

■ **This is a strange obstruction** – a drop of water over the lens of my underwater point-and-shoot. A handy tip is to spit on the lens and then water won't stick to it!

■ **This picture** was taken through railings, and the lens is obscured by a railing that I couldn't see through the viewfinder.

Lab problems

THE LAST COUPLE OF SHOTS *I'm showing you don't really fit in anywhere else since they are the fault of the lab. They're still worth looking at, so you'll know what they are if you see them among your pictures.*

■ **The white line** *around this swan was caused by a hair that was left in the printing machine at the lab. The negative will be fine so just ask for a free reprint.*

■ **This unsightly stain** *is a drying mark on the film. You could have it touched up in Photoshop, but ask your lab for a new film for free.*

A simple summary

✓ On a point-and-shoot camera, what you see is not quite what you get. Bear that in mind when framing your compositions.

✓ Being aware of the focusing limitations of your camera will help you to overcome them.

✓ Opening the back of your camera before the film has been finished and rewound will ruin your pictures.

✓ Don't shoot into the direction of the sun, windows, or mirrors. Take a few steps to one side.

✓ You won't necessarily see something that is obstructing the lens through the viewfinder, so check there's nothing in the way.

PART THREE

GIVE IT SOME ART AND SOUL

THE ARTY STUFF

BEFORE YOU READ THIS SECTION, I would just like to underline a few important points. Firstly, the word "arty" is sometimes used almost as a derogatory sneer. Don't accept that. *Arty is inspirational* and is at the core of the best of us, both as people and as communities.

Don't listen to outside voices telling you that you're not artistic. More importantly, don't listen to your own inner voices telling you the same thing. Just because you haven't previously expressed yourself creatively doesn't mean you're not a *potential artist*. Of course you are. The bottom line is that you will certainly produce more interesting pictures than you do now if you get into the arty stuff, and you'll get *a lot more satisfaction* from your work. So get out there and be arty!

Chapter 10

Natural Light

A S A PHOTOGRAPHER, it's important for you to understand what sorts of effect different types of light will have on your pictures. Even if you ultimately decide to use only studio light for your work, you should know that natural light is the inspiration for almost all artificial effects. As such, it's important to study natural light first. Whether you are using window light for a portrait, or sunlight to create a silhouette, I hope this chapter will point you in the right direction.

In this chapter...
✓ Light is everything
✓ Times of day
✓ Window light
✓ Using the weather

THE LIGHTING EFFECTS FOUND IN NATURE CAN BE AWE-INSPIRING

Light is everything

OUR CHOICE TO TAKE A PICTURE OR NOT *is decided by subject matter. Or is it? We have all had the experience, at one time or another, of walking down a street, or driving through the countryside, on a dull, grey day when we wouldn't dream of taking a picture. A few hours later, on our way home, the late afternoon sun has broken through and thrown a golden glow down the street or flushed the west side of the hills and we are now feeling rather frustrated that we don't have a camera with us.*

In cooking terms, if subject matter is the raw material of a meal, then light is the magic ingredient. It's the spices, the sauce, and the Dom Pérignon.

Think consciously about light. When do you use window light? What do you use strong, harsh light for? What is back-lighting good for? These are the sorts of question you should start asking yourself.

Even if you think you will use artificial light only, both in and out of the studio, it's important to study natural light first.

Light thinking

To transform your photographs from being simple visual records into exciting, satisfying images you need to understand daylight. The different qualities it has at different times of the day and how weather affects the photographic quality of light is important stuff and essential knowledge for the photographer.

The angle at which daylight hits a subject is critical, so you need to bear in mind the following points:

1. It affects the shape of the object it is falling on, or more accurately the apparent shape of the object

2. It affects the texture that the camera can reproduce

3. It affects the picture composition through its manipulation of tonal balance (this is particularly true in black-and-white photography)

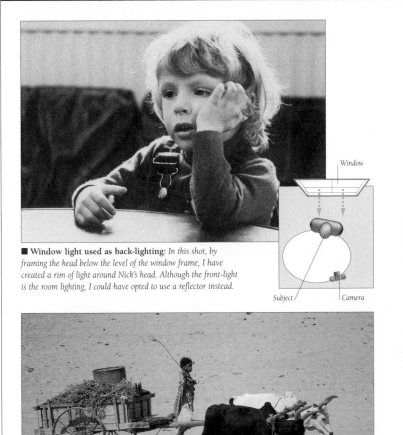

Window

Subject / Camera

■ **Window light used as back-lighting:** *In this shot, by framing the head below the level of the window frame, I have created a rim of light around Nick's head. Although the front-light is the room lighting, I could have opted to use a reflector instead.*

■ **Midday with the sun directly overhead** *is not ideal for portraiture because the face ends up in the shade. It is, however, good for hard-edged colour or subjects with strong shapes.*

129

■ **This is a classic** *window-light portrait. I turned my son Nick so that he was three-quarters on to the window. This is so easy to do and the results are lovely. However, be careful with your background: I removed a picture and just used the plain wall.*

■ **Here I used** *a large gold reflector to bounce the strong Mojave Desert sunlight into the face of former Tears for Fears star Curt Smith. Note the way the gold light tints the picture. I also like that you can see the reflector mirrored in his sunglasses.*

Looking creatively at light

Most lighting set-ups are reproductions of natural lighting conditions. And to make accurate images we need to be able to use the equipment creatively. All technical decisions in photography are also creative decisions, so light needs to be considered almost as much of a creative device as composition, lenses, shutter, and aperture (all of which are coming up in the next few chapters). When you understand how all of these function, you can get them on your side and greatly affect the look of your pictures. (Later on, I will also dip into visualization, which I trust will help you to look at everything around you a little differently.)

Times of day

IT'S IMPORTANT *when you are beginning to study light that you first understand how light changes as our little planet circles around the sun. It is also a good idea to take the time to learn which subjects are best suited to certain times of the day.*

No doubt you will have noticed that the quality of daylight changes throughout the day. That's partly because the *colour temperature* of the light changes. This change in colour temperature alters the colour balance of your pictures so that if you photograph your house at sunrise it will appear to be a different colour than if you had photographed it at noon.

> **DEFINITION**
>
> *The colour of light, or **colour temperature**, is calculated in degrees Kelvin (° K). For example, midday is between 5200 and 5400° K. Colour temperature readings can be taken on a colour temperature meter, and from this reading you can work out what you require in terms of filters or camera/lens settings to get your desired colour effect.*

■ **These two pictures** *demonstrate how light can transform a subject in the space of just a few minutes. The shot above was taken in dull, overcast light. Just moments later the autumnal sun arrived to work its magic, making the stag really glow.*

SAME TIME, DIFFERENT VIEWPOINT

One of the great things about natural light is that, even if you stay seated in the same spot, you can find totally different effects just by turning in a different direction. These two photographs illustrate my point. Admittedly these weren't taken at exactly the same time, but there was only a moment between them.

■ **In this shot** *the mid-morning light bouncing off the sea in the Seychelles has gifted me with a silhouette.*

■ **A few minutes** *later, in the same lighting conditions, I had the kids run from the other side of the beach. When daylight is at a lower-than-noon angle (i.e., before 11 a.m. or after 2.30 p.m.), it can be used as a back-light, sidelight, or front-light.*

Film manufacturers balance the emulsion of their colour films to produce accurate colours when used with either natural or artificial light. The changing of the sun has a dramatic effect on light and shade – or, in more photographic language, the highlights and shadows on a subject – throughout the day. Therefore, a landscape, or even a face, will look entirely different depending on the time of day at which it is shot.

There is now a huge range of colour-correction filters available. These are made of gelatine and come in various sizes. Using these, you can manipulate the existing light into almost any colour you want. They are coded using WRATTEN numbers. WRATTEN 4Y, for example, is a very pale yellow and WRATTEN 40M is a strong magenta filter. However, many photographers prefer to rebalance the colour of their pictures later using manipulation software on a computer.

Don't worry too much about colour balance when you are shooting colour negative, or print, film. Any unfortunate colour casts can be corrected later in printing.

Window light

THE FAITHFUL OLD WINDOW has been the traditional light source for painters and photographers for centuries. Don't underestimate it or take it for granted – window light can be very versatile.

When shooting by window light remember that you are using natural daylight and that the colour balance will therefore change with the time of day.

The window light is my favourite portrait light, as it has been for many photographers. Most of us own a window, so that's one less thing to go out and buy!

If you are using a point-and-shoot camera, don't turn on the flash when trying to capture window light – it will destroy the light's quality.

Sometimes, on a dull day, it may seem that the window light is too low for photography, but that is just because you are more familiar with brighter outdoor light. Indeed, there may not be a lot of light, but it can nevertheless be of a beautiful quality and all you need are a tripod and a long exposure.

If you are working with a tripod you don't necessarily need fast film. Try using slow, very sharp film for its inherent intense colour saturation.

■ **Professional photographers** *go to great lengths to reproduce window lighting for food, but you can't beat the real thing. The classic still-life light has the window behind the food and about 1 metre (3 ft) higher.*

133

I have always felt that flash attracts so much attention that it's impossible to take really natural or fly-on-the-wall reportage pictures with it.

At this point I think it's only fair to tell you that *available-light* photography is not so easy on a point-and-shoot. This is because the maximum aperture of the lenses is smaller than on SLR cameras. But that's not to say it can't be done.

If you are attempting available-light photography on a compact camera, remember that the wide-angle mode lets in four times as much light as the tele mode because it works at a larger aperture. So stay on wide-angle.

Available-light photography is at its moodiest in black-and-white. I recommend that you really look at those low-light situations... and turn off the flash.

> ## DEFINITION
>
> **Available light** is *a term used to describe photography utilizing existing light only. Often available-light photography refers to pictures taken in low light. Many of the most moving and powerful reportage photographs ever taken have been available-light pictures. Unfortunately, too many photographers seem to have lost the art of this type of photography and allowed the flash to take over. With the fast film available today, there is virtually no situation that cannot be photographed without flash.*

■ **Even though it's night-time** *it doesn't have to mean flash! I took this picture on Bonfire night. The bonfire gave me plenty of light, and it's the firelight that's injected the atmosphere.*

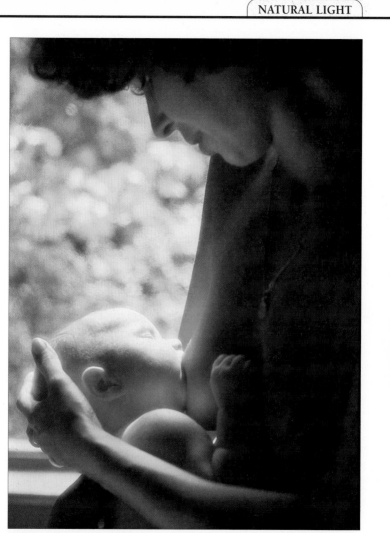

■ **I have used the window light** *as back-light in this picture. Note that I have exposed just for the highlights – the baby's face – and not used a reflector to lighten the shadows. I wanted a moody feel.*

135

Using the weather

WEATHER HAS JUST AS DRAMATIC AN EFFECT *on light quality as time of day. Many great pictures have been made on a stormy, black-clouded day. It is sometimes on those days that seem so unsympathetic to photography that a shaft of light can burst through and create a magical effect.*

As with time of day, you need to be aware of the photographic potential of different weather conditions so that you can anticipate possibilities. The last thing you want to do is find yourself saying something like "I wish I had my camera, but it didn't look like a very nice day."

■ **I love stormy, black-skied days for landscapes** *because this is the sort of thing that can happen. A spotlight has burst through the clouds and lit up the Grand Canyon. I even got a rainbow thrown into the bargain! It's not worth the risk of packing your camera away on days like these — you may regret it.*

I always keep two plastic shopping bags and some rubber bands in my camera bag. Then, if it rains, I cut a lens-diameter-sized hole in the closed end of the bag and fasten it around the lens with the rubber band. This enables me to look through the opening of the bag, keeping the camera dry.

■ **One of the greatest** *things about rainy days is the way the light bounces off all the shiny, wet surfaces.*

A simple summary

✓ Light is possibly the single most important factor in your decision to take a photograph.

✓ The way an object looks – its shape, texture, and colour – is greatly affected by the angle at which it is hit by light.

✓ In many cases artificial lighting is set up to replicate the effects that are found with daylight.

✓ Midday has a colour temperature of 5200–5400° Kelvin.

✓ Film is manufactured to produce accurate colours at noon in daylight.

✓ You can change the look of a scene by using colour-correction filters over your lens.

✓ Window light has long been the favourite light source of photographers and painters.

✓ Even bad weather can offer great photographic opportunities – so it pays to be prepared.

Chapter 11

Artificial Light

THERE ARE BASICALLY TWO DIFFERENT light sources available to the studio (or indoor) photographer – tungsten and electronic flash. Tungsten light provides continuous light; the sort of lighting we have in our homes is tungsten. And we are all familiar with electronic flash; it's what you find on a point-and-shoot camera, but the studio version is many times more powerful. Both of these light sources have their advantages, and many professionals who earn their living in the studio use both systems.

In this chapter...
- ✓ *Before you start*
- ✓ *Tungsten light*
- ✓ *Electronic flash*
- ✓ *Dedicated flash*

ALTHOUGH IT'S NOT EXACTLY KIDS' STUFF, ARTIFICIAL LIGHTING NEEDN'T BE TOO TAXING

Before you start

OKAY, BEFORE WE GO ANY FURTHER *I want to say something. Having a good understanding of daylight, or natural light, is a solid basis for learning to artificially light your pictures. Whether we're talking flashguns, studio flash, or tungsten light, I believe it makes sense to try to reproduce your favourite daylight effects inside with artificial light.*

I am of the opinion that, for the rookie lighting director, it is easier to start off with tungsten lights. With these, you can see exactly what you're doing and they are also cheap to buy or construct. You use the camera meter exactly as you do for daylight. I would suggest you start a file of your favourite lighting-dominated pictures that you've pulled out of magazines. Try to work out how they were lit and then copy them. Have fun!

Reflector   Floodlight   Reflector

Reflector

Subject   Reflected light

■ **For this still life** *I bounced the light off a large white card placed 1.5 metres (5 ft) from the subjects. Another white card opposite acted as a reflector to fill in the shadow. I used an 82A filter to convert tungsten light to daylight and shot on slide film.*

Tungsten light

THE FIRST ARTIFICIAL LIGHT *that photographers worked with was tungsten light. Hollywood's great cinema photographers in the golden age of black-and-white films perfected the use of spots and floods to create the glamour we associate with that period. We have never surpassed those lighting set-ups. In fact, many will say we have never matched them either. However, still photographers learned their lighting skills from Hollywood and created those great film-star portraits.*

There's a whole generation of young photographers making retro Hollywood portraits at the moment. Tungsten has the great advantage that what you see through the lens is what you get on the print. It's much easier to see the effects you are creating than it is with electronic flash (unless you are very experienced). Tungsten light is also cheaper to buy and the exposure will be handled through the camera's metering system as with daylight. Many portrait photographers still prefer tungsten for black-and-white photography (myself included). That is because the warmer colour of the tungsten light has the effect of improving skin tones. It lightens darker spots and creates a smoother texture in almost the same way as using a light orange filter with flash does.

■ **This is classic** *Hollywood lighting: just one spot 1.2 metres (4 ft) above the camera. A piece of fine stocking across the lens makes an excellent soft filter. Combine the two to give a Rita Hayworth look to your lady friends.*

■ **A simple** *portrait light typical of a window light. This is actually bounced off a white umbrella, but card would do just as well. You could also use your flashgun for this set-up.*

Trivia...
When I was a young photographer I tried to use every light in the studio on every picture. These days I usually use just one light source with reflectors.

141

EFFECTS OF A SINGLE LIGHT SOURCE

I shot this series to show you the dramatically different effects you can have on a face just by changing the angle of a single light source, in this case an ordinary old mirror-back flood. Note how the shape of the face seems to change as I moved the light.

■ **For this first shot,** *I positioned the light just above the camera.*

■ **The position** *of the light for this shot was about 1.2 metres (4 ft) above the camera. It gives a slightly darker look.*

Quartz lighting

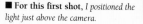

Most modern spots and floods use quartz lights. Quartz lights are compact and can produce a high wattage with much less heat than traditional tungsten lamps.

Never move quartz lights while they're switched on. They are very delicate and could explode.

INTERNET

www.phototechmag.com/
previous-articles/sept99-
kerr/kerr1.htm

This article, "Controlling Light for Photography" by Norman Kerr, gives some great analysis of what can be achieved with just one studio light.

Quartz lights are expensive and the lamps themselves are fragile and expensive (bad combination), but they're definitely much cooler (temperature-wise) to work in (especially for the model) when in a confined space. They are also ideal for location work because you can fit a whole studio's worth of lights into one small case.

Never attempt to change a quartz bulb using your bare fingers. The moisture on your fingers will damage the coating and the bulb could explode. Always use a tissue or gloves.

■ **Here the light** is coming in at a three-quarters angle from approximately 2 metres (6 ft) above the camera.

■ **To hide half** of the face in shadow I placed the light at head height and directly to the side of the face.

■ **I achieved** this look with the light placed about 60 cm (2 ft) off the ground directly in front of the camera.

Electronic flash units

IN RECENT TIMES, *electronic flash units have become the main light source used in professional studios, and this is because of two major properties. Firstly, the light is balanced to daylight film; this means that the photographer is guaranteed perfect (as in natural) colour balance on every frame. And secondly, the flash duration is so short – between $\frac{1}{400}$ and $\frac{1}{3000}$ of a second – that the photographer can freeze movement automatically to get a sharp picture.*

Most 35mm SLR cameras will synchronize with a flashgun on $\frac{1}{200}$ of a second or slower.

Always check your shutter-speed setting when you are working with flash to ensure that your camera will synchronize with the flash. Also note, though, that you should never set your shutter at faster than its recommended sync speed. You will end up with a blank film.

■ **I used a professional studio-type flash here**, *but if I'd been near a big window, I would have used that instead. I bounced a flash into a white umbrella and hung tissue paper over the brolly to soften the light. The larger the area of your light source, the softer the light will be, and vice versa.*

Floodlight

Tissue paper

Diffused light

Subject

Umbrella

Reproducing daylight

Most often, photographers use flash systems to reproduce daylight effects, and usually the flash is diffused in some way, maybe by being bounced out of a white (or sometimes silver or gold) umbrella or by firing it from behind a translucent plastic sheet or tissue paper. There are many methods but almost always the aim is to reproduce window light in its many forms. Flash units produce spotlights, fibre-optics, dim headlights, strip lights, semi-lights, and more, but we are trying to reproduce the light that we have seen in nature.

The large studio flash systems and the portable systems (they all have their own trade names: monoblocks, monolights, compact systems, for example) have built-in tungsten guide lights. These guide lights are on a dimmer switch connected to the flash power switch and get brighter and dimmer as the flash power is increased and decreased.

LIGHT METER

Your camera's meter cannot measure the flash output of studio flash units; you need a separate light meter.

The guide lights give a pretty good indication to the photographer of how the flash picture will look. However, most photographers shoot Polaroids® to help them gauge how their final picture will look.

Most medium-format and all large-format systems make a Polaroid back or Polaroid holder so photographers can shoot an instant guide without changing cameras. At least one company also makes them for 35mm cameras.

■ **This is the sort** *of flash set-up that you would expect to find in a professional studio. There's really no need for the casual photographer to invest in something like this.*

elinchrom

Dedicated flash

THE MAJOR CAMERA MANUFACTURERS now produce
dedicated flashguns. These are extremely
sophisticated pieces of kit – they can do almost
anything but wash your car! These flashguns
work with the camera to produce a wide range
of flash effects, and they can even be used to
enable autofocus in the dark.

DEFINITION

A dedicated flashgun is
one designed by camera
manufacturers to work only
with their own cameras.

Trivia...

My first professional studio
flash unit was a second-hand
French model (probably
fifth-hand really). I couldn't
afford white umbrellas, so I
painted ordinary umbrellas
with white emulsion. They
looked decidedly uncool but
worked pretty well!

■ Here I wanted to blur the
runner to give a feeling of speed,
but freeze him also to see the
action. I lit him with tungsten light
and took a meter reading. The
shutter was set to half a second to
get the blur, and two flash units
(one each side of the runner) fired
at the end of the half-second,
freezing the movement.

147

I can't tell you how to operate your flash technically in this book because each system is different. You need to study the manufacturer's instruction book.

Buy a TTL (through-the-lens) metering remote cord with your flashgun. This enables you to physically move the flash off the camera while still maintaining all the dedicated features.

This means you can use it as a single-source light for the studio, a back-light or sidelight, or you can diffuse it or bounce it. And you still have automatic exposure. Great stuff!

Using dedicated flash outdoors

I use my flashgun to alter existing light balances outdoors. For example, I will make the foreground lighter in relation to the background. Prior to the advent of dedicated flashguns, this was a tricky calculation. But now I can tell the flashgun what I want to achieve and presto!

■ **To change the existing tonal balance** *of this scene, I used my camera's dedicated flash. It's a very simple procedure. With the flash set on automatic, I set the camera at -⅔ of a stop, resulting in a darker, less distracting background, but one that is still readable.*

You can, for instance, set the flash for correct exposure and set the camera to underexpose by 1 stop (half the normal exposure). That way you'll end up with a correctly lit foreground (most often a portrait) and a dark (but still readable) background. Check it out!

Don't assume your dedicated flash is like your old flash. You must really study the instruction book or you could make mistakes.

INTERNET

**www.photography.about.
com/arts/photography/
library/weekly/aa
122099.htm?terms=
Home+Lighting**

*This is a useful article in
About.com's photography
pages on how to photograph
celebrations, parties, and
other events that take place
in an indoor setting.*

A simple summary

✓ Before learning about artificial, or studio, lighting, you should first ensure you have a good knowledge of natural light.

✓ Tungsten lighting was the first type of artificial light that photographers ever worked with.

✓ Tungsten lighting is good to work with because it looks the same on a print as it does in life.

✓ Quartz lights are able to produce a large amount of light with much less heat than traditional tungsten lamps.

✓ The main light source used in professional studios is the electronic flash unit.

✓ Flash systems are usually used to produce a daylight effect.

✓ Dedicated flashguns are high-tech flashes produced by manufacturers to work only with that same brand of cameras. They can be extremely versatile.

Chapter 12

Lens, Aperture, and Shutter

I'VE ALWAYS HAD A PROBLEM with teaching methods that separate technique from creativity. So many books split them up, as if you need to have a split personality to be a photographer – a technical you and a creative you. In fact it's all one and the same. I know plenty of photographers who master the technical side but can never express themselves creatively. In part, I think it's because they don't realize that the technical decisions they make when taking a picture are also creative ones. In this chapter I want to show you how to make creative use of your camera's most fundamental elements.

In this chapter...

✓ Lenses – what can you do with them?

✓ Using filters

✓ All about aperture

✓ Getting to grips with shutters

YES, YOU CAN SLOW DOWN A WATERFALL!

Lenses – what can you do with them?

LONG LENSES AREN'T DESIGNED SOLELY to get you closer to your subject; nor are wide-angles only used "for getting more in". They both have inherent characteristics that we can exploit creatively.

Telephoto lenses compress the perspective in a photograph. That means they give the effect of pulling the background up closer to the foreground. With very long telephotos (500–1000mm on a 35mm camera), the foreground can look almost like it's pasted on to the background, and mountains that are hundreds of miles away can appear to be

LENS EFFECTS

I'm using this series of pictures here simply to illustrate how a change of lens can mean a very different interpretation of the same subject. The understanding of this lesson is the beginning of getting a new grasp on creative photography.

With each of these pictures, not only have I changed lens, but I've also moved back away from the model to keep her the same size in each shot.

INTERNET

www.amateurphoto.about.
com/hobbies/amateur
photo/library/bllenses.
htm?terms=lenses

This page has some good information on lenses as well as tips on filters.

■ **This first picture** *was taken with a 24mm (wide-angle) lens, which exaggerated the distance between the model and the monument.*

right next to each other. You won't really notice a pronounced compression of perspective on a compact camera, but it will still be noticeable enough on, say, a 135mm zoom to give you a considerable compositional change from the wide-angle setting.

Modern lenses have a coating that has considerably reduced the flare you used to get when back-light hit the lens.

■ **This Grand Canyon picture** *was shot on a 300mm lens. The escarpments appear to be almost pasted together although they are hundreds of metres apart. The perspective has been compressed.*

■ **The 105mm lens** *has pulled the monument closer to the model than our eye sees it. This is the same as most point-and-shoots on tele setting.*

■ **The 300mm telephoto lens** *has pulled the monument much closer than the eye sees it. The girl now appears right next to the background.*

Selective focus

Another very important quality of telephoto lenses is that
the longer the lens, the shorter its inherent depth of focus.
Remember that you control the potential depth of focus of
each lens with the aperture. The ultimate in potential *selective
focus* is a telephoto lens that is wide open. So, telephoto
lenses can be used to manage colour (or tones if you're
shooting black-and-white) and perspective.

> **DEFINITION**
>
> *When you focus on one plane
> and throw the rest out of
> focus by using a large
> aperture, this is called*
> **selective focus**.

■ **These shots were taken** with a 35–105mm zoom at 65mm. The first one was stopped down to f16 to
produce front-to-back sharpness; for the second one I opened up to f3.5 to selectively focus on the glass.

*Photographers often use the term short lens to describe a wide-
angle lens and long lens to describe a telephoto. This refers to
the focal length of the lens.*

The wider the angle of the lens, the greater its depth of focus, and the
greater its ability to exaggerate perspective. For example, if you focused
a 20mm lens at about 2 metres (6½ ft) and stopped it down to f16, everything
would be sharp from about 10 cm (4 inches) from the camera to infinity. Even with the
aperture wide open it is difficult to see the effect of selective focus with a wide-angle lens.

In fact, it's almost negligible on an 18–24mm lens. So the wide-angle lens can be used to produce exaggerated perspective and hard-edged colour compositions.

Zoom lenses

The zoom lens can produce a little graphic touch all of its own. Use a longish shutter speed (say between ⅛ of a second and 1 second), then zoom from wide-angle out to telephoto during the exposure, and you'll get the effect shown here. Quite fun really!

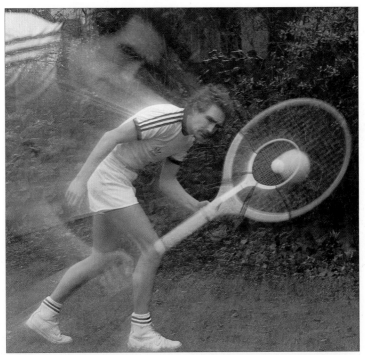

■ **I made this photograph** *using a 35–70mm zoom lens stopped down to f22, so I needed a slow shutter speed (¼ of a second) to compensate. I used a tripod and the model remained perfectly still. I started the exposure with the lens set at 35mm and zoomed through to 70mm in approximately ⅛ of a second. The last half of the exposure was at 70mm. These timings are approximate. You will see that the speed of your zoom will affect the look of movement in your pictures.*

Using filters

ALTHOUGH PHOTOSHOP®
*can produce any effect that an
on-lens filter can (and more), many
photographers still prefer to use
traditional filters on their cameras.
That is because they want to visualize
the effects in the viewfinder. That
way, they can produce an effect
more in harmony with the subject
in front of them.*

SCENE SHOT WITH NO FILTER

Filters for colour film

For colour work there is a huge range of
filters that are not for special effects but
that are used more subtly, just to fine-
tune the colour. You may want to make
the skin tones a little browner, or the
sunset a bit pinker, or make the whole
scene just a touch bluer. To do this sort
of work you use colour-correction filters.

SHOT WITH 2A WARMING FILTER, TO INTENSIFY COLOURS

■ **The effect you see here** *is the result of simply
breathing on the lens on a cold day. I like the
feeling it gives more than any soft-focus filter –
and it's easier on your pocket.*

■ **I jazzed up the colours** *in this shot by using
a 2C filter, a darker version of the 2A. Other
warming filters that would do the same job are
the 81 series (A–EF) or the KR series (1–15).*

Professional photographers carry a large selection of colour-correction filters in their camera bags. The other type of filter that the travel photographer never leaves home without is the polarizing filter, which works in a similar way to your sunglasses. By cutting down the reflections on surfaces, the polarizing filter enables you to reproduce more saturated colours in your pictures. For example, it creates dark blue skies with white cloud formations (if there are any clouds, that is).

Graduated filters

The other family of filters that's very useful to colour photographers is that of the graduated filters. As the name implies, they are coloured at the top and graduate to clear at about halfway down. This allows you to manipulate the colour in half of the picture while leaving the rest of the shot as it is. Some good examples of this would be to make a grey sky blue with a blue grad, or create a sunset effect by using a pink grad. Who said the camera never lies?

■ **I used a blue grad here** *to make a grey sky blue. Note that the sheep and grass in the bottom area are unaffected because the bottom half of the filter is clear.*

SUGGESTED COLOUR FILTERS

The list below is just a small selection of the filters that are available. These are some of my personal favourites; I think they are worth trying out.

Type	Colour	Effect
Polarizer	N/A	Creates more saturated colour
81A and 81C warming filters	A pinkish brown	Skin tones, saturates most colours
Blue grad	Half blue, half clear	Blue skies
Pink grad	Half pink, half clear	Sunsets
Neutral-density grad	Half grey, half clear	Darkens area without altering colour

Filters for black-and-white work

Colour-correction filters are also very important in black-and-white photography. They are used to manipulate the tones in an image. They do this by lightening the tones at their own end of the spectrum and darkening the tones at the other end of the spectrum. So, if you shot a red kite in a blue sky using a red filter, you would produce a black-and-white print with a nearly white kite in an almost-black sky. The polarizer and the grad filters are also valuable for black-and-white work. They do basically the same job as on colour film. Give them a try and see what you think.

■ **A typical red-filter** *black-and-white picture. The filter has darkened the blue sky and, in so doing, has given more emphasis to the clouds.*

SUGGESTED BLACK-AND-WHITE FILTERS

Here I have listed some of my favourite filters for black-and-white work. You can use others, of course, but I find these are the most useful.

Type	Effect
Polarizer	Cuts down reflections, similar effect to sunglasses
Orange	Darkens blue skies, clears up skin blemishes
Red	Same effect as the orange but to a greater degree
Yellow-green	Lightens the tones of foliage
Infrared (almost opaque)	Maximizes the contrast between light and dark tones
Neutral-density grad	Darkens the whole area without altering tonal contrast

SPECIAL-EFFECTS FILTERS

There are literally hundreds of special-effects filters that you can buy to add an endless degree of creativity to your pictures. I would suggest you search through the Cokin and Hoya catalogues to see what tickles your fancy.

■ **The soft-focus** *filter has given this London scene a romantic, foggy atmosphere.*

■ **The starburst filter** *turns every source of light into a star.*

■ **A rainbow filter** *on this picture has thrown a rainbow effect across the sea.*

■ **Using the split-image filter** *here has made one solitary candle appear as though there are many.*

All about aperture

THE APERTURE CONTROLS THE DEPTH OF FOCUS in the *photograph. The smaller the aperture (the smaller the hole), the greater the depth of field will be; the larger the aperture, the shallower the depth of focus. This means that if you want a picture that is sharp from foreground to background you need to stop down to a small aperture.*

Stopping down will provide you with sharp, hard-edged colour (or tones, if you're shooting in black-and-white), so you'll need to consider every line, angle, and colour carefully in the viewfinder because once they are hard-edged they will affect your composition. But if you want one part of the image sharp (maybe a portrait face) and the background out of focus, you need to open up the aperture.

INTERNET

**ubmail.ubalt.edu/
~dhaynes/photo/depth.
htm**

This web page contains an article on depth of focus from Introduction to Photography *by David Barnes.*

■ **For this shot,** *because I was using a 200mm tele lens with its inherent short depth of focus, I needed to stop down to f22 to hold sharpness from the foreground to infinity.*

APERTURE

As I said earlier, the aperture controls the volume of light that enters through the lens to expose the film. However, its creative job is to control the depth of focus of the lens. By controlling the depth of focus, you control where the emphasis is in the picture. I have used this series of shots to demonstrate how you can use depth of focus to tell your story.

■ A **50mm lens** *stopped down to f16 has kept both the girl and the background sharp. I am showing you both the girl and her environment.*

■ **Now that I have opened up** *to f5.6, the shorter depth of focus means I am placing more emphasis on the girl.*

■ **Now I am wide open at f2** *and your eyes are drawn to the girl because the background is completely out of focus.*

Using aperture creatively

The creative effect of aperture is most apparent on colour and tone management. When the aperture is wide open, the out-of-focus colours will merge together into a soft background, and the out-of-focus foreground becomes a soft-coloured frame for the sharp object that is the point of focus. Black-and-white tones are softened and merge at the edges. Open up the aperture when you want the viewer to concentrate on the object you've focused on, and stop down when you want the viewer to take in every detail of the picture, from foreground to background. If I was, for instance, shooting a portrait of a famous gardener I would probably stop down to show the garden as well as the gardener.

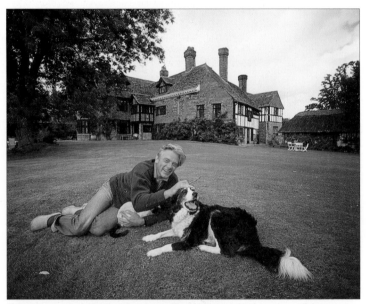

■ **It was important to me** *that I kept the man, his dog, his cat, and his house sharp. All those components are important because they are evidence of what kind of man he is. I used the ultimate depth-of-focus combination: a 20mm wide-angle lens stopped down to f16.*

■ **In the composition opposite,** *I wanted the viewer to see only the girl, so I used a 180mm tele lens wide open at f2.8. The out-of-focus trees have been made into a soft, sympathetic background that adds to, rather than detracts from, the picture.*

Getting to grips with shutters

THE SHUTTER IS THE PART OF THE CAMERA *that controls the amount of movement in the resulting photographs. This is because the longer the shutter is open, the more light the film in the camera is exposed to. This has important creative applications.*

The fact that a fast shutter speed freezes a moving object means that, graphically, it holds that object sharp and hard-edged in the picture.

All the colours (or tones, if you are working with black-and-white film) will be well defined. A slow shutter speed will blur the subject and give an entirely different graphic look to the picture: the colours and the edges of forms will merge together, and the emotional impact on the viewer will be entirely different to that from a fast-shuttered image.

SHUTTER SPEEDS

This series of pictures shows you the effect that the shutter has on movement. Once you understand the creative role of the shutter you really can add another dimension to your photography. By using the shutter creatively it's possible to further express how you feel about a subject, not just record what it looks like. And that's what we are all aiming to achieve.

■ **The cyclist was travelling** *at a normal road speed when I shot this picture. The camera was stationary and the shutter speed was 1/500 of a second.*

You can also use a slow shutter speed on static subjects and let the camera move through the exposure to produce an almost surreal image.

A photographer friend of mine has so many hangovers that he always shoots on a fast shutter speed just to avoid camera shake!

■ **Shot at ¼ of a second,** *the sparkler has exposed a beautiful arc against the black background, which is essential to the success of the picture. Try some really slow shutter speeds – they can be wild!*

■ **I panned with the bike** *for this shot taken at ¹⁄₃₀ of a second. The cyclist is fairly sharp and the background has an interesting movement streak to it.*

■ **I kept the camera still** *and shot on a shutter speed of ⅛ of a second. There is a real feeling of speed about the shot.*

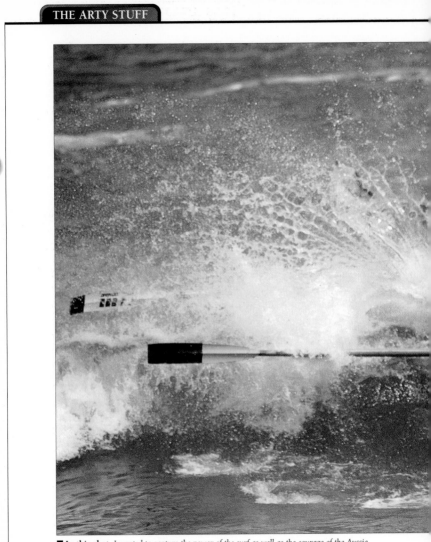

■ **In this shot,** *I wanted to capture the power of the surf as well as the courage of the Aussie lifesavers. The ¹/₂₀₀₀-of-a-second shutter speed has frozen every drop of the action.*

■ **This beautiful, slow-shutter-speed picture** *of a bullfight was taken in Spain by my wife Michelle. The ½-second shutter has merged all the colours together. It looks just like a painting.*

Making a choice

As with all so-called technical decisions in photography, the *aperture priority* or *shutter priority* decision is, most importantly, a creative one.

If you have a 35mm SLR, don't let the camera automatically set the shutter–aperture combination. Make a creative choice.

I often shoot action on a fast shutter speed and then later think, "Maybe this picture would've been more interesting if I'd used a slow shutter speed and blurred the movement." Try to shoot moving subjects with both fast and slow shutter speeds and see which result you find most pleasing.

DEFINITION

Aperture priority and **shutter priority** *are modes on semi-automatic cameras whereby you select the setting for one and the camera automatically sets the other. I'm using it here to emphasize the need to make a creative decision regarding one or the other.*

A simple summary

✓ Telephoto lenses compress the perspective in a picture – that is, they make the background seem closer to the foreground than it really is.

✓ The term selective focusing means to focus on one plane (that is, one distance from the camera) and keep everything else out of focus.

✓ A wide-angle lens is often called a short lens; a telephoto lens is a long lens.

✓ The wider the angle of the lens (that is, the lower its millimetre value), the greater its depth of focus.

✓ Your creative use of lenses can be increased through the addition of colour-correction filters.

✓ Filters come in many different colours and effects, and they can be used successfully for both colour and black-and-white photography.

✓ The depth of focus in a photograph is controlled by changing the lens aperture: the larger the aperture, the greater the depth of field, and vice versa.

✓ When the aperture is wide open, out-of-focus colours merge together to form a soft background.

✓ The shutter speed dictates for how long the film is exposed to light.

✓ Using a fast shutter speed when photographing a moving subject will freeze the subject in the picture.

✓ A steady camera combined with a fast-moving object and a slow shutter speed will result in a blurred image.

169

Chapter 13

Learning to See

I T ALWAYS SURPRISES ME just how little of their world people actually see. Obviously I don't mean "see" as in being aware of, I mean it in a more all-absorbing way – the difference between seeing and looking, if you like. If you want to be able to take interesting pictures, first you have to learn to see them. In its most basic form, that can be a commitment to not always shooting from your own eye level. But there is so much more to it than that. In the next few pages I'll be giving you some essential advice on making interesting images.

In this chapter...
  ✓ The alternative point of view
  ✓ Beauty out of the mundane
  ✓ Colour management
  ✓ Colour thinking

TAKE THE TIME TO REALLY LOOK AT THE WORLD AROUND YOU

The alternative point of view

AN ALTERNATIVE American photographer named Ralph Gibson made a great series of pictures over a long period: using a normal 50mm lens on a 35mm camera, he shot everything from just 60 cm (2 ft) away. The result was a very powerful vision of his world that was fresh and exciting. A Coca-Cola® bottle sitting on a Harley-Davidson can say "USA" just as much as the Statue of Liberty. Other terrific examples of alternative points of view that spring to mind are an Irving Penn portrait of Miles Davis consisting solely of Davis's left hand and a Richard Avedon portrait of Muhammad Ali that was just his fist.

What I am trying to say is that there is always another way of taking a picture – a fresh approach, a less obvious, and therefore surprising, image that will have a great impact on the viewer. Ask yourself the question "How else could I make this picture?" Sometimes it won't work, but that doesn't matter; the times when it does work will give you a big buzz.

INTERNET

www.artisdead.net

This site contains not just photography, but a range of work from several fields of the arts. There are often some very interesting photographs here, so check it out!

■ **Sometimes a mere section of the subject** *can tell the story in a more interesting way than the whole thing. To me, this shot undeniably says "USA".*

Vertical or horizontal?

On the subject of alternative viewpoints....
We all know that most cameras take
rectangular pictures, of course. But how
many of us consciously decide which
way round to turn the camera when we
are about to take a picture? "Vertical or
horizontal?" is a question you should
ask yourself every single time.

*Always have a look at your
subject before you shoot.
Don't automatically take
a horizontal picture.*

■ **I was struck** *by how beautiful this
guardsman's helmet was. I used my
80–200mm zoom to crop in tightly.
Look hard for the alternative picture:
it's always there, you just have to find it.*

■ **By shooting from such a low camera angle** *I was able to remove all the
distracting foliage from behind these girls and use the sky as my background. I
took this picture with a 24mm (wide-angle) lens with a red filter to darken the sky.*

Trivia...
*There's a scene in the film
Dead Poets Society in which
the teacher (played by Robin
Williams) makes the whole
class stand on their desks to
view the room from a different
angle. This symbolic gesture
reflected his philosophy on
life in general.*

173

Beauty out of the mundane

EVERY DAY WE WALK PAST *mundane, even ugly, things. Living in the 21st century, many of us are increasingly confronted by neglected "stuff", usually discarded by our fellow citizens. But is it really all ugly and worthless? I suggest you take a closer look, just as Irving Penn did in the 1970s when he held his controversial "Street Material" exhibition at the Metropolitan Museum of Art in New York. The pictures are of old cigarette butts and rubbish that he picked out of the gutter and shot with uncompromising clarity in the studio.*

At the time, many critics slated Penn's images, but I think they are masterpieces and very beautiful. So don't be too ready to discard the trash and the seemingly mundane – take a fresh look at it instead.

Personally I've always been fascinated by the graphics created when pop posters on wall boards are torn and become multilayered designs in their own right, sometimes as exciting as many highly acclaimed abstract paintings. I call this ripped-off art. Here's a couple of mundane subjects that I hope will point you in a different direction.

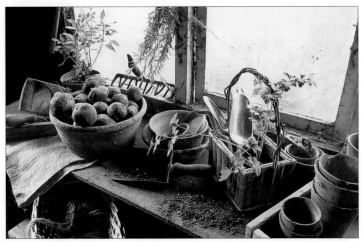

■ **The beautiful window light** *coming in from behind this would-be still life has brought these rather mundane subjects to life and made a worthwhile photograph. Open your eyes to the possibilities around you.*

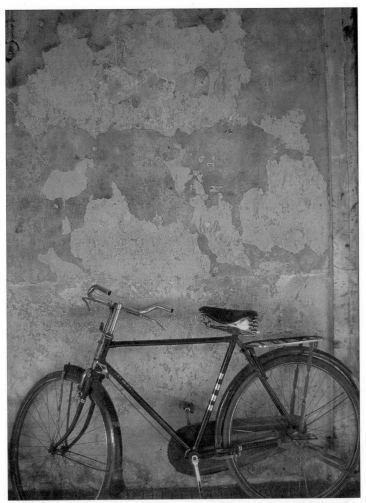

■ **It's just an old bike** and a neglected wall in Goa, India, but I love both the colour and the composition. Forget about the actual objects and try to see just the shapes and colours.

■ **Perhaps** *an inner-city rubbish dump is not the most obvious of places to find beauty, but this photograph is a personal favourite of mine. There are some great potential pictures that we walk past every day – we just need to be alert to the possibilities.*

Trivia...

As I was taking this photograph at a dump, the site caretaker approached me from behind and asked me what I was up to. I told him him I was taking a picture. "What the hell for?" was his response, and he walked away throwing his hands up in disbelief. He was amazed that I could find something worthy of a photograph among all that rubbish.

Colour management

OUR EMOTIONS *are deeply affected by colours. Different colours and different combinations of colours produce different emotional responses from us, or rather in us. Unfortunately, not many photographers use this knowledge in their colour work. Ultimately, at the highest level, the style of a photographer working in colour develops and becomes individually recognizable because of his or her own responses to colour.*

We are all individuals and we will all be attracted to different colours and colour compositions.

We know that cool colours (blues and greens) can have a calming effect on highly strung people while at the same time having a depressing effect on people of a depressive nature. Hot colours (reds, oranges, yellows) have a stimulating, positive effect on laid-back people, but can prove rather too stimulating and heighten the spring of tension in violent people.

The density and contrast of your colours will be considerably affected by exposure. Underexposure, or highlight exposure, produces saturated colours and high contrast. Overexposure, or shadow exposure, produces washed-out colours and soft contrast.

Here are a few examples of thinking in colour, where colour management, rather than the subject matter, has created the mood.

■ **I planned** *this shot of a spice market in Singapore because I wanted to produce a warm sepia tone to the picture. This is a good example of colour management. Don't just let colour happen.*

INTERNET

www.thirdeyephoto.
com

*The great Third Eye
Photowork Collection
web site exhibits many
photographs shot from
unusual points of view.*

■ **It was the harmonious arrangement** *of greens that caught my eye in
this scene. The French fisherman plays second fiddle to the colour. The more
you work on your colour awareness, the quicker you will improve.*

■ **By creating a blue photograph,** *I have added to the melancholy atmosphere of the picture. Think
carefully about what you are trying to say when you begin introducing colours.*

Colour thinking

WHEN YOU ARE setting up portraits or still-life pictures, it's very important to be aware that every colour you introduce will influence the mood of your picture. Experiment with background and colour combinations to see what moods you can create. This is the only way to learn what the end results will be.

When shooting on location, train your eye to become increasingly selective. Look at objects as coloured or tonal shapes, animate and inanimate, rather than what they actually are. For example, a red lorry parked next to a green field is a red rectangle against a green background. You can then ask yourself, "Where will I place that red rectangle?" instead of thinking, "What a gorgeous truck, I must take a picture."

■ *This picture is all about seeing colour; it wouldn't be interesting in black-and-white. The joy of shooting colour lies in finding the patterns that are all around us.*

The pop artists of the 1960s, such as Andy Warhol, left behind some great examples of how to create mood through the use of colour. Photographic images were often the basis of their paintings.

Don't just throw colours into your picture because they look nice; be selective and manipulative with your colour selection.

■ *The deliberate use of these hot colours gives this inanimate subject a feverish, sexual feel.*

■ **In spite of all the incredible colours** *available to us, this is one of my favourite pictures. The tulips of Amsterdam are a great sight – a real symbol of spring. And I found this yellow tulip to star in my shot.*

A simple summary

✓ Always look for the most interesting way to depict your subject. To find the most interesting viewpoint you need to take the time to look for it.

✓ The things we see every day can still be worthy of a photograph – even the ugly stuff! Cast aside your preconceptions and take another look.

✓ The colours you choose will produce emotional responses. Use them wisely.

✓ Colours can be used to convey a feeling almost regardless of the subject matter.

✓ Think of subjects as coloured shapes from which you must build an appealing design.

Chapter 14

Space and Composition

I THINK OF PHOTOGRAPHIC COMPOSITION as a secret knowledge – almost subversive, a "them and us" kind of thing. Most people looking at photographs believe they are being emotionally moved only by the subject matter of the picture, and to a large degree they are: they are made sad by a picture of starving children, or joyful by a picture of a snowball fight, for example. But they are unaware that the composition of the photograph also has a powerful influence on how they interpret the picture. The photographer can exercise an almost subliminal influence over the viewer, who is getting a message but doesn't know how the photographer is delivering it.

In this chapter...
- ✓ *Thinking composition*
- ✓ *Here are the laws!*
- ✓ *Photographic composition*
- ✓ *Creating visual effects*

LET THE SPACE FLOW INTO YOUR VIEWFINDER

Thinking composition

THE TRADITIONAL LAWS *of composition were passed down to us by painters, but with the advent of the camera they started to evolve. And they have continued to evolve along with the camera. Compositional awareness (or the lack of it) is what ultimately separates an average photographer from a very good one – that's what I believe. The ability to compose your pictures well will empower you to take pictures that capture how you feel about a subject and to pass that feeling on to the viewer.*

Trivia…

In the early days of my career I composed my pictures based on whether they looked nice or not. It was not until I worked with graphic designers that I learned the rules of composition and my photography improved dramatically.

So the early photographers borrowed their compositional structures from painters. Well, kind of. In fact, many of the early photographers were painters experimenting with a new high-tech medium. The compositional structures of traditional art were formed without the benefit of the optical variations that we photographers have today. They couldn't visualize a landscape painting through the wide-angle of a telephoto lens, so it was not until photographic optics grew sophisticated enough that it became possible to manipulate perspective.

This development of photographic lenses resulted in a compositional feedback. In the second half of the 20th century, photographers started to influence the compositional form of painting, instead of the other way around. In the 1920s, the *Surrealist* artists came along and broke many of the old painterly rules. They took objects and put them together in new and startling ways. It is worthwhile checking out the Surrealists because some of their compositions are very exciting and there is much to learn from their outrageous (at the time) images.

It's very important to know about a few of the classic laws of composition because they can form a solid basis for you in your work.

Don't just snap away – always think of your composition before pressing that button!

DEFINITION

*The **Surrealists** created paintings, drawings, and photographs that were inspired by dreams. Salvador Dali, Pablo Picasso, and Marcel Duchamp were the leaders of the movement. Man Ray was the most famous Surrealist photographer.*

Here are the laws!

I DON'T LIKE TO BE BOUND BY LAWS, nor *do I wish you to be, but there are some basic compositional pointers that you would do well to adhere to. Even if you ultimately decide you want to go with your own ideas, please give these a try first!*

INTERNET

www2.southwind.net/ ~tkalp/pw2/Comp.htm

This page of Wichita South High School's web site contains some sound advice and information on photographic composition.

The law of thirds

Divide your frame into thirds both horizontally and vertically, as illustrated, so that you have nine equal-sized parts. The law of thirds states that the four points where the lines intersect are the strongest points in which to place the most important feature of your picture.

■ **The height of the wave** *and the direction the surfer was facing led me to place him at the top left intersection on the rule-of-thirds grid that is etched in my brain. He just wouldn't have looked as good at any other point in the frame. Try placing your subjects at all four intersections and see the difference.*

185

Positive and negative shapes

Positive and negative shapes are more obvious and more easily recognized in black-and-white. The positive shapes are the main features, or the subject matter, and the negative shapes are the shapes between and around the main features of the picture. The dynamics of the picture are as dependent on the negative shapes between and around (to the edge of the frame) the main subject or subjects as they are on the positive shapes.

■ **In this picture,** *the white space (the negative shape) between the figures is just as important to the graphic impact of the photograph as the shapes of the figures (the positive shapes).*

The golden triangle

The rule of the golden triangle is based on the equilateral triangle, and it's mostly used in the composition of portraits. The triangle is a powerful form and can be placed anywhere in the frame. The triangle will form the positive shape and the background and/or foreground will be the negative shape around the triangle. The geometric strength of the triangle provides the subject of the portrait with its strength and is a dynamic starting point when learning to compose portraits.

■ **When you first start** *taking portrait photographs I would suggest that you try to use the golden triangle rule. It's a very strong, tried and tested compositional form.*

Photographic composition

HAVING LAID DOWN A FEW LAWS, I will move on to what I would describe as photographic composition. It's all to do with space management in the viewfinder and it's not about highfalutin stuff like art and graphic design. It's about placing the subject in your viewfinder to tell the story as effectively as you can.

I used to keep a file of favourite photographs and paintings that I had torn out of magazines, and I admit I copied the compositions – it was a great learning experience. We can all learn from the masters.

During the learning process, you'll inevitably make compositions that don't work very well but that only shows that you're trying. Anyway, your compositions will evolve to be different from mine or anybody else's – you will develop your own style. So be outrageous, be bold, try being different!

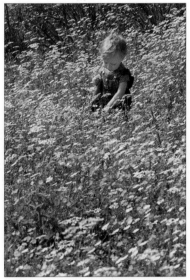

■ **For this composition** *I went with my common sense. I used the space in my viewfinder to tell a story. By making the boy small and keeping him in the top half of the frame, I have illustrated the billions of wild flowers that cover Majorca in the spring.*

Leaving a space

Many of the seemingly spontaneous compositions that we see in reportage photographs are not grabbed shots but, in fact, very well planned. Some of the great pictures of Henri Cartier Bresson are good examples. He often made compositions in the viewfinder, leaving a space for a figure, such as a cyclist, to fill, and then pushed the button when the cyclist appeared in that allotted space. So try composing and waiting; see if it works for you. (You can, of course, direct someone into your allotted space!)

Check out the patterns

Keep your eyes peeled for the patterns all around. You can isolate these to make exciting pictures. Here's a couple of examples to point you in the right direction.

■ **These vineyards** *and rape fields have man-made patterns that were just waiting there for me to isolate a small section for my picture.*

INTERNET

www.photography bygarrett.com

This is my own web site. Why not visit and see if there's anything you like?

■ **This great array** *of plates was in the Savoy Hotel's kitchen when I arrived, but the pattern only revealed itself to me once I looked down from up a ladder. I used an 18mm (wide-angle) lens to exaggerate the perspective.*

Creating visual effects

ONCE YOU'VE LEARNED THE LAWS of composition and you've started looking for patterns and leaving space in your pictures, you can start to consider other compositional effects. There's a whole host of options available to you and in the next couple of pages I'll take you through some of my favourites.

Symmetry

A symmetrical composition is a well-balanced composition in which the visual feel or the shapes on one half of the picture are echoed on the other. In general it has a calming effect on the viewer. But, on the other hand, it's usually not very dynamic.

Frame within a frame

I think that introducing a second frame into the frame of your photograph is a useful tool to create uncertainty and a touch of surrealism. This is a good device for making the viewer think about the picture a bit more.

■ **By photographing these men** through a huge piece of piping I have placed them inside a circle, thereby creating a round composition within the rectangular 35mm frame.

Scale

By introducing some element of known size into a picture we can get across dynamically just how big or small our subject really is. But we can also use scale to create an optical illusion and trick the viewer into believing the picture's subject is much smaller or bigger than it really is.

Repetition of shapes

A faithful old standby is the use of repeating shapes. You often see this compositional form combined with good use of perspective. A good example is a Victorian London terrace where the repetition of the columns makes a satisfying pattern.

■ **A classic standby for photographic composition** *is the repetition of shapes. These trees work very well, creating an aesthetically pleasing pattern.*

Eliminating space for a reason

By cropping right in on the head in a portrait and eliminating any "breathing space" around the person, you can create a feeling of tension. The person's face is almost trapped in the picture by the edges of the frame. They have, in a sense, nowhere to go, and the effect can be one of claustrophobic tension. Try this out for yourself. Also try shooting a few frames where you loosen the framing and leave some space around the face. You will notice the difference in graphic tension.

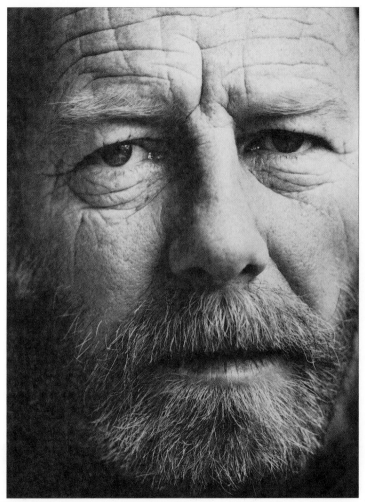

■ **Artist Wes Walters** *is a very intense man, and I have tried to convey that by framing very tight on him. I have eliminated any space from around him. This type of clamped-in composition adds tension to the picture.*

Space and movement

The position in which we place a moving subject in our frame has a profound influence on the viewer. If the runner has just entered the frame on the right and there's a lot of space on the far left, you will give the impression that the runner has a long way to go. If, however, you compose with the runner on the left and about to leave the frame, he seems to be at the end of his or her journey.

■ **The boys in the water** *seem to explode out of the picture; this adds to the feeling of the power of the waves and to the excitement of their play. Don't be afraid to try unusual compositions – it's how you learn.*

Focal point

Try to use the focal point in a very simple way at first. Take an open, featureless picture and then introduce your focal point to it. It may also serve as a scale reference. A small focal point will make a dramatic difference to your pictures.

Technically, the focal point is the area of the picture on which the photographer focuses. With regards to composition, we are referring to the object in the picture that attracts and holds the viewer's eye.

■ **The use of a focal point** *is beautifully demonstrated by comparing these two road shots. You can get a much better sense of scale in this second picture. I think you'll agree that it was worth waiting for the car heading towards Death Valley.*

A simple summary

✓ The laws of composition are long-standing and awareness of them is vital to the creation of good photographs.

✓ The law of thirds shows that there are four key points in your frame, one of which should contain your picture's most important feature.

✓ The golden triangle law, often used in portraiture, urges you to create an equilateral-triangle shape within your frame.

✓ You should aim to include important shapes between the subjects of your composition just as much as you aim to create good shapes with the subjects.

✓ You can learn a great deal about composition by trying to copy some of your favourite artists' photographs or paintings.

✓ There are many visual effects you can utilize to make your pictures more informative, appealing, or just plain weird. These include using symmetry, a second frame, and scale.

✓ The focal point is what you want the viewer to look at.

PART
FOUR

SOME PICTURES MIGHT COMBINE SEVERAL THEMES

PHOTOGRAPHIC THEMES

ONCE YOU HAVE A GRASP of the basics of photographic techniques, the next step is *applying* this knowledge to specific subjects. I have grouped the subjects into the classic themes of photography. This section is aimed mainly at you rather than at your equipment. It is about how you as a person learn to see the world as a photographer. It's about becoming more *visually aware*, and it's also about simplifying photography.

I want you to be able to take great pictures without making a big deal about it. I want you to *experience* the joy that I've had taking pictures, without some of the hassles and goof-ups that I've had on the journey. You'll still make mistakes but, hopefully, not nearly as many. And anyway, the great shots you get – and you *will* get some great shots – will draw you back to photography time and time again.

Chapter 15

Portraits

THE OLD SAYING "Never judge a book by its cover" cannot apply to the portrait photographer. In fact, the exact opposite approach is required: we must learn to observe the cover because it's all we have. I believe the visual evidence presented by a subject is an accurate map of what was and is going on inside the person – the personality or character of the person as it were. The lines on the face of an old man have been earned during a long life; the tension in the hands, and general body language, betray what is being felt beneath the surface. To become a good portraitist you must develop your observation skills so you can capture the essence of the people you photograph.

In this chapter...

✓ Putting your subject at ease

✓ Types of portrait

✓ Black-and-white vs. colour

A GOOD PORTRAIT REVEALS THE SUBJECT'S INNER SELF

Putting your subject at ease

THE GREAT AMERICAN PHOTOGRAPHER Richard Avedon said
of his portraits, "They are also pictures of me, of the way I feel about people."
I certainly agree that portraits can reveal as much about the photographer as
they do of the subject. I also know from personal experience that if we make
an effort to photograph our friends, family, or clients sympathetically and with
some style, we can give them a great deal of pleasure.

I spent the early years of my career as a fashion photographer, and I was amazed
to find out that these beautiful and supremely confident models were
so vulnerable and nervous below the surface. It just goes to show that
we are all scared of having our portraits taken.

*One of the most essential skills for portraiture is the ability to put
your subject at ease. And in order for you to be relaxed enough to
make your subjects relax, you need to be on top of your technique.*

■ **It often requires** *some effort on your part to bring out your sitter's personality. These two shots of
Sir John Betjeman are good examples. We were having a serious discussion about poetry when I took the first
picture. The second shot (the next frame, in fact) shows his response to a joke I made about one of his poems.*

You need to be ready – to have planned where (if on location) and how you are going to take the portrait. Have the camera loaded and with fresh batteries. Even if you are nervous – and you will be at first – try to look like you know what you are doing. Make your subject feel they are in safe hands. If you are using lights, have them set up in advance. I would suggest you use somebody else to sit in while you set up the lighting. I have discussed lighting in detail in chapters 10 and 11, so have another look at those for some lighting suggestions. However, I will emphasize here that those dull, overcast days that seem useless for most photography can produce soft, flattering light for portraiture.

■ **This shot was taken** *on a dull, overcast day. As you can see, it produced a sympathetic light for the sheep farmer. A 135mm lens shot wide open (f2.8) has added a soft, out-of-focus background.*

Music and conversation

If you are shooting indoors or in a studio environment, try putting on a little background music. Music is a great soother of nerves. But be sure it's nothing too heavy – that can have quite the opposite effect. If you have a large selection of music at hand (and this is not a bad idea), ask the sitter if he or she has any preference.

Give the impression that you have all the time in the world for the shoot. If your subject wants to sit and chat, sit and chat – and use the time to observe the sitter.

Most of the portraits you take initially will be of family or people you know, so you can steer the topic of conversation to one they enjoy, where they feel safe. Be prepared to take plenty of pictures, two or three rolls, and keep talking while you are shooting. The expressions the sitter makes when answering your questions can make magic pictures.

Let the sitter know that you are taking lots of shots. This eases the pressure for that "one good picture" (it takes the pressure off you too) and helps your subject to relax a little.

If you think about it, with people you know you can pretty much predict what sort of expressions they will make for any question you ask them. That way you can shoot a variety of expressions – the laugh, the smile, the frown, and so on.

POSING AND CAMERA ANGLES

The number-one tip I can give you for posing a portrait sitter is to have them lean towards the camera. Although the body language is far more dynamic when they are leaning towards you, many portraits are taken with subjects leaning away.

Don't just let portraits happen. Be in charge and tell the sitter how you want them to pose. They will be grateful because they are probably too self-conscious to know what to do themselves.

Since most of us, whether amateur or professional, are trying to flatter (or at least please) the subject with our portrait, we need to know how to deal with the usual human frailties.

a) If a man is going bald, shoot from below the chin line and use side lighting (never top or front lighting).

b) If your subject has a double chin (or two), shoot from slightly above head height and have them stretch forwards and look up at the camera.

c) Many people display their nervousness by tensing up their mouth. Ask them to fill their cheeks with air and blow it out again – hard. This relaxes the mouth and makes them feel so silly they almost always laugh: there's your great happy portrait.

■ **Christina thought** *I'd gone completely mad when I asked her fill to her cheeks with air and blow a raspberry! But it did relax her and she did laugh.*

200

d If the subject has a long nose, have them look straight at the camera (with their head straight) and use as long a focal length as possible. The long lens (tele mode on a point-and-shoot) will compress the perspective, making the nose look shorter.

e Some people stare when they are nervous. Just quietly ask them to close their eyes and lower their chin to their chest. After a few seconds get them to slowly lift the head and open their eyes as they do. Stare gone – magic!

f To produce a dynamic, "I'm-the-governor" portrait, shoot from about chest height looking up at your sitter. The sitter can keep his head still and just look down at the camera with his or her eyes. I shoot most of my corporate portraits like this.

Trivia...
The great portraitist Yousuf Karsh was making a portrait of the larger-than-life British prime minister Winston Churchill, who was smoking a cigar as usual. But Karsh was having problems getting Churchill's trademark British Bulldog expression. Legend has it that the photographer suddenly jumped out from behind his camera, snatched the cigar from Churchill's mouth, and stuck it between his fingers. Churchill was furious and glared at the camera, thus creating a very famous portrait.

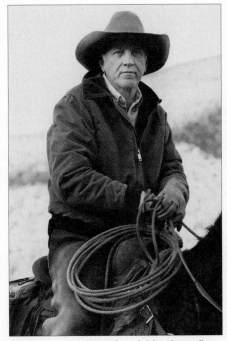

■ **By looking up at this cowboy** *I feel that I have really captured his natural authority, which so impressed me when we met in the mountains of Colorado.*

Choosing clothing and backgrounds

Generally, I like my sitters to dress in very plain, unpatterned clothes, especially for head-and-shoulders shots. Anything that will distract the eye from the face has to go. Sparkly earrings can be very distracting, for instance. However, having said that, if your favourite aunt just wouldn't be herself without her floral dress, beads, and ostrich-feathered hat, then that's what she must wear.

I also think it's important to keep the backgrounds really simple on formal portraits. You can buy large sheets of great coloured papers in speciality paper shops, but I like to spray boards with pressure-pack paints. You can make clouds or matted effects that are atmospheric but that don't distract from the face of your sitter – after all he or she is the focal point of the portrait.

■ **I don't usually like to distract** *from the face with patterned clothing. But, let's get real, Auntie Flo just wouldn't look the same in a black dress, now would she?*

Types of portrait

THERE ARE MANY DIFFERENT TYPES *of portrait, of course, but they can be squeezed into two main families: the environmental portrait and the cosmetic portrait. We will look at each of these in detail in just a moment, but first of all it's important to understand how they differ.*

Probably the type of photographic portrait most of us are familiar with is the cosmetic type. This is a picture in which the sitter is the sole subject, and there may be very little of anything else in the shot. This sort of photograph might be used by an actor, for example, to put with his résumé when looking for work.

An environmental portrait, on the other hand, is about more than just the physicality of the sitter. The world that the sitter inhabits is also of great importance. An example here might be a farmer with either his land or his farm animals in the background.

INTERNET

www.photography.ca/
otherartists/karsh.html

*Have a look at this web page
for a handful of portraits by
Yousuf Karsh, as well as a
brief biography of this
important portraitist.*

Environmental portraits

Taking portraits of people in their own environment is great because the background and props show us who this person is – their interests, taste, or lifestyle are also in the picture. This is an ideal situation for the wide-angle lens (or the wide-angle mode on a point-and-shoot camera).

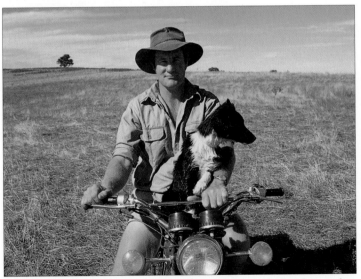

■ **This is a good example** *of an environmental portrait. It was important to me that I show not only this tough Aussie farmer and his sheep dog, but also the land that made them tough, so I shot it with a 28–70mm zoom lens set at 30mm and stopped down to f11 to keep the background sharp and clear.*

You need to be very careful when posing your sitter on location, however. Find a suitable place in your viewfinder and make sure that the subject's head is clear of lampposts, doorknobs, and anything else that may end up looking like horns or other appendages.

If you are taking photographs indoors, have a look at the ambient lighting before you automatically turn on the flash. It may be low but it could be of a beautiful quality.

Try using a tripod, turning off the flash, and asking the sitter to stay still while you make a long exposure.

■ **This portrait** *was shot in a dimly lit café in Italy, with my camera supported on my camera bag. The exposure was ⅕ of a second. Using a flash would have killed the moody lighting – and it would have also disturbed the subject.*

Cosmetic portraits

Since a cosmetic portrait is intended to show the sitter in a flattering fashion, you need to be able to achieve that goal. In this section, I'll give you a few useful tips to help you on your way.

As a general rule, focus carefully on the eyes. They are, after all, the windows of the soul.

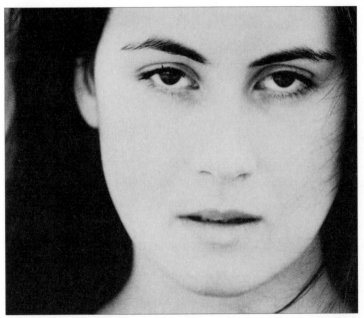

■ **For cosmetic reasons,** *I used an orange filter over the lens for this photograph, simply to hide the fact that it was one of those blotchy-skin days.*

If your subject has blotchy skin or acne, I would suggest using black-and-white film (400 ISO) with an orange filter. If the acne or blotches are very pronounced try using a red filter. The filter will absorb the red in the blotches and produce a clearer skin tone. (If you have a point-and-shoot, you can try holding the filter in front of the lens, or in front of the flash if you are using it.) A soft-focus filter will also help: this can also be very flattering for ladies of "a certain age". Try finding one that is only slightly soft.

Portraits by candlelight are very flattering. The flickering directionless light is soft and produces a warm glow. Generally speaking, the longer the lens the more flattering a close-up portrait becomes. But bear in mind that lenses over 200mm are quite unmanageable.

Never push a wide-angle lens in close to a face (unless you don't like the person!) – you will just get an elongated head and a long nose.

If your sitter has bags under the eyes or dark eye sockets (I'm describing myself here!), place a silver reflector on the table – cooking foil works fine – and have them lean over it. The silver reflector bounces light back up and fills in the dark eye sockets, removing much of the baggy look. It also puts a bright highlight in the eye, which gives the sitter a bit of a twinkle. God knows we all need a bit of a twinkle now and again!

■ **I used a silver reflector** *on the table below business tycoon Richard Branson to bounce some light up into his eyes. It added the visionary sparkle that I was looking for.*

Black-and-white vs. colour

THAT OLD CHESTNUT AGAIN. *I personally prefer black-and-white portraits to colour portraits. There, I've said it. I think that when we are talking glamour shots of young starlets or perhaps the portrait of your daughter in her prom dress, then colour does the job nicely. It can have a glossy look and, obviously, if you have a particular special dress or whatever that you want to record for posterity, colour is the only choice.*

But I believe that most people look better in black-and-white than they do in colour. They seem to carry a greater authority and strength. On the other hand you might think that is a load of old rubbish! It's all a matter of taste.

■ **I chose black-and-white** *for this shot of actor Julian Holloway because I feel that black-and-white is stronger for portraits, especially male portraits. I threw a black scarf around him to remove any distractions from his face, and I cropped off his balding head for obvious reasons (sorry, Julian!). This was shot on a 6 x 6-cm Hasselblad, and the medium-format neg has produced a complete range of tones.*

A simple summary

✓ Before you can even begin to shoot a portrait you must be able to put your subject at ease. This is an important skill of the portrait photographer.

✓ Some soft background music will help relax most people.

✓ Friendly chatting is not only relaxing but also helps you get to know your subject a little better.

✓ Ensure your sitter's clothes aren't too garish – unless such attire is very much part of the subject's personality or character.

✓ Learn how best to flatter your subject. Different faces require different angles and techniques.

✓ Choose relevant backgrounds for environmental portraits – and beware of false appendages!

✓ I believe that most people look better in black-and-white than in colour. You may not feel that way. Try both and see which you like.

Chapter 16

Landscapes

OF ALL THE CLASSIC THEMES in photography the one that leads to the most disappointments is the landscape. Friends often show me their holiday pictures, and when we come to a landscape shot they say, "I don't understand this one – it just didn't come out like it looked." What has happened is that they didn't know how to turn an inspiring view into a landscape photograph. When we survey a scene, our eyes dart around picking all the most attractive features and reassemble them in the brain as a perfect landscape picture. A camera can't do that – it only records what we point it at – not the majesty of the full scene.

In this chapter...
- ✓ Landscape tradition
- ✓ The importance of light
- ✓ Choosing your film
- ✓ Point-and-shoot landscaping
- ✓ Think comfort

Landscape tradition

PAINTERS HAVE THE *great advantage over us snappers that they are able to manipulate their landscape. They can move a tree from here to there or even remove an unsightly outhouse altogether. But the basic principles that govern them govern us as well. The traditional rules were that a foreground leads the eye towards a focal point and that the eye is held in the picture by a background. And the dominant ingredient was, and still is, light.*

Photographic composition

Early photographers relied entirely on painterly composition, and they continued to do so – through lack of choice – until the development of wide-angle and telephoto lenses. However, with the wide-angle lenses photographers were able to exaggerate perspective, while the telephoto lenses were able to condense perspective and isolate a section from the landscape. In a turn of events, 20th-century painters became more influenced by the compositional techniques used in photography.

The classic foreground–focal point–background composition is still the basic form for landscape photography. However we must also search the views in front of us for patterns, using the lenses we have at our disposal. Forget how you feel emotionally about the patterns and concentrate on finding them.

You may end up with an incredibly simple picture of just a rock in front of cumulus clouds but the print could capture the emotional feeling you had for your whole surroundings.

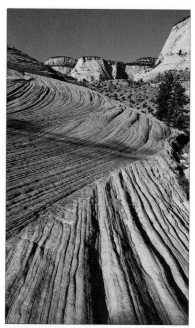

■ **Using a 24mm (wide-angle) lens,** *here I was able to make full use of the swirling rock formations at Zion National Park. Notice how all the lines in the picture lead your eye towards the cliff faces in the background.*

■ **The plains of the Serengeti desert** in Kenya seem to go on for ever, and it can be difficult to get a sense of scale. That's where a focal point – such as these trees I found – comes in very useful.

What is a focal point?

When I refer to a focal point the sort of thing I am looking for is an isolated farmhouse in the middle ground or a great lone tree or horse... or a boat in the middle of a lake. Do you get the idea?

A focal point is something towards which you want the viewer's eye to be drawn – something that stands out from the rest of the frame.

Where do I find a pattern?

By "patterns" I mean things like ploughed fields, or the different-coloured crops planted side by side, or a range of hills picked out with your telephoto lens. Some landscapes combine both of course: if you are really lucky (or alert) you may find a farmer ploughing those aforementioned fields with a flock of birds in his tail.

If you have running water in your picture (like the sea or a waterfall), choose a slow shutter speed (between ⅟₁₅ and 1 second) to give the water a soft, milky, fluid appearance, contrasting any rocks surrounding it.

The importance of light

THE QUALITY OF LIGHT *falling on a landscape dramatically influences the patterns and form of the end photograph. Traditionally, early morning and late afternoon provide the most dramatic lighting effects. However, heavy, dark-clouded skies can also suddenly be broken by a shaft of light at any time of day, and those conditions often provide great landscape potential.*

■ **Landscape photography** *is dominated by light effects. This Australian scene was captured during a brief pause on a stormy day. The black clouds are there, but light has smashed through to highlight the trees.*

Light is a fleeting thing and a great effect is often only present for a few moments. You need to work fast sometimes, so keep a loaded camera and tripod ready. If carrying a tripod is just too much of a hassle – you like landscapes but not *that* much! – try one of those mini tripods that you can set on a rock or brace against a tree.

I find a compass useful when I am in a beautiful place and the light is boring. I set the compass and, by calculating where the sun will rise and set, I get a feel of how the shot will look in early or late light. I can then plan to be in the right spot at the right time.

If your camera has overexposure compensation (+ or -), bracket the exposures from -2 and through to +2. You will then have pictures where you have exposed for the highlights (-2) as well as shots where you have exposed for the shadows (+2). You can decide later which effect you prefer.

Choosing your film

I LIKE TO EXPERIMENT with different types of film for landscapes. If I am shooting a subject that I feel needs to be very sharp, and where I want to reproduce every detail perfectly (like an old tree stump or a rock formation), I usually shoot with slow film, a 100 ISO. At other times I use very fast film for a grainy effect. You can create the look of an Impressionist painting with 1600 ISO colour, while 3200 ISO black-and-white can give the look of an old etching.

I can't really tell you what film to use. It's down to your personal creative choice to dictate your selection of film. Try out as many types as you can afford and see which ones produce the results that you like best. After all you are taking photographs that will appeal, first and foremost, to you, aren't you?

Whatever type of film you choose, a polarizing filter is the ideal companion for shooting landscapes. It will increase contrast, therefore darkening blue skies and really bringing out the cloud formations.

■ **A polarizing filter** is a great tool for use in colour landscape photography. By cutting back the reflected light for this shot (in the same sort of way that sunglasses do), the sky has become a deeper blue, so the clouds appear whiter and stand out more.

Black-and-white

Having said that film type is a personal choice, I will say that I am totally hooked on black-and-white for landscapes and I thoroughly recommend you to have a go too. It will take time before you start seeing colours in terms of tones (we'll look at that in Chapter 22). Obviously you can increase your black-and-white enjoyment level by doing your own printing too, but these days minilabs do a good black-and-white service.

■ **Here I used** *an 18mm (very wide-angle) lens to play around with the perspective. I put a red filter over the lens and it has worked magic on the sky.*

Of course, the greatest landscape pictures aren't taken from a public viewing post. Nor are they the result of just popping out of the car and taking a couple of snaps. They are the result of hard graft and dedication.

■ **The early morning light** *over this Scottish loch was very intense so I fitted a red filter to a 28–70mm zoom set at 60mm, and I waited for the sun to go behind the clouds to avoid flaring. In this kind of situation, add 2 stops to avoid underexposure.*

■ **Just an old dirt road**, *some cumulus clouds, and a tiny truck – you don't need many elements to make a satisfying image. Again, the red filter has done a great job on the sky. Keep it simple. Less is more.*

To get shots of that calibre you'll have to walk for miles with your camera kit and tripod, having risen from your bed 2 hours before dawn to make sure you capture the dawn light as it hits the landscape.

I don't want to put you off already, but by understanding what makes a landscape and being prepared to make a bit of an effort (without going over the top) you can improve your pictures immensely.

The filters that go with a black-and-white landscape are orange and red. Orange will darken the blue sky (making for a darker grey, that is) and a red filter will make the blue sky almost black with white clouds.

You have no doubt seen many good Ansel Adams landscapes using those filters.

INTERNET

www.photography.
about.com/arts/
photography/library/
weekly/aa071999.htm

"Who's Ansel Adams?", you ask! Well this is as good a place as any to find out.

Point-and-shoot landscaping

THERE IS NO REASON why you can't shoot good landscapes with your point-and-shoot. All the same principles apply regardless of which camera you use. You simplify and you have to be aware of the need for dramatic light.

If you have a zoom lens don't use it just to save some walking. As we discussed in Chapter 12, you can use your lens creatively – not just to get more in on the wide-angle or get closer on the telephoto setting. Your wide-angle will exaggerate the perspective, which is great on cloudy skies, for example, and your tele will compress the perspective pulling the background mountains up closer to the boat on the water, for instance. You can also use the telephoto to isolate the patterns you have spotted inside the view that you are looking at.

■ **The stormy sky in this scene –** *shot on an APS with a 28mm fixed-focal-length lens – really makes this picture. But the composition is a classic painterly one. The foreground rocks lead your eye to the road, and the road takes you to Monument Valley's famous monoliths. The tiny car makes a good focal point.*

Many point-and-shoot cameras have a panoramic facility built in which can look great on landscapes. But remember that you still need the same compositional disciplines.

Think comfort

I DON'T THINK THERE IS ANY OTHER photography theme that rewards effort as much as landscape does. To take really good landscape pictures you need to be up before the rooster and home after the nightingale goes to sleep. You sometimes need to walk all day and it is often too hot or too cold. In the light of this, I reckon that your comfort is as important as your photographic eye and technique.

Make it easier on yourself

You can't – or at least I can't – take good pictures if you're cold, hot, or tired. I can't walk if my feet are sore or if I am fed up with having a sunburnt neck. Although you can't control the weather, there are some basic steps you can take to ensure your comfort level is as high as possible. Once all your personal needs have been cared for, you will be free to shoot masterpieces. The following list contains some of the points that I think are essential for any landscape-photography trip.

- Wear a shirt that has a collar
- Always take a hat: these are essential in both hot and cold climates
- Wear good waterproof hiking boots with thick socks
- Take energy bars to eat
- Carry a full water bottle
- If it's sunny don't forget your sunblock
- Take a torch in case you get lost and you need to find your way in the dark
- A space blanket is useful if you need to keep warm, and it folds down to a very small size
- Take a mobile phone in case of emergency
- If you are driving remember to landmark your car: park it near a huge tree or rock, for example – it's easier to get lost than you might think
- A compass will help too (but don't leave it in the car!)

WATERPROOF HIKING BOOTS

COMPASS

■ **Here's another shot** *of Monument Valley – this time from a different camera position. I isolated the monuments using a tele lens and used a pinkish filter to exaggerate the colour. In addition, a neutral-density graduated filter darkened just the sky.*

A simple summary

✓ The classic landscape picture has a foreground, a focal point, and a background.

✓ A focal point is something to which the viewer's eye is drawn.

✓ Look for patterns in the frame to add some texture to your photo.

✓ Light is arguably the most important element of landscape photography.

✓ Experimenting with different films is the only way to find out which you prefer, leading you to make informed creative choices.

✓ The same landscape principles apply regardless of whether you are using an SLR or a point-and-shoot camera.

✓ Consider your personal comfort when you are setting off on a landscape-photography trip.

Chapter 17

Still Life

STILL LIFE IS THE PHOTOGRAPHIC THEME that allows us the greatest amount of control. We choose the objects to be photographed, the background, the lighting, the film, the lens, and the camera angle. We create the composition by just moving objects around. Still life is the closest that photographers get to painting a picture. I find that, when I turn to still life, I have to slow myself down to enjoy the contemplative process. Once you get into it you will find that it's rather therapeutic. In this chapter, I'll discuss the qualities a still-life photographer needs and pass on some tips that the professionals use in creating images.

In this chapter...

✓ Getting inspired

✓ Considering your viewpoint

✓ Composition

✓ Light and colour

✓ A word to the wise

YOU CAN FIND INSPIRATION IN THE MOST ORDINARY OF OBJECTS

Getting inspired

I THINK THE BIGGEST OBSTACLE we all encounter when it comes to still life is not knowing where to start, that is, not knowing what to photograph. A good place to start is by studying the old masters.

Take a look at works by painters such as Matisse, Chardin, and Cézanne, and photographers like Penn, Kertez, Man Ray, Miro, and Meatyard. Study their compositions, their balance of colour, and their lighting. You can also gain inspiration by studying the objects that they chose and thinking about why they chose them.

The sincerest form of flattery

Don't be embarrassed by copying (or trying to copy) old masters. It's a great way of learning, and if you are knowledgeable of your art history you will find a number of famous photographic still lifes that are in fact copies of – or perhaps I should say "inspired by" – old paintings.

Props and the squirrel mentality

Most still-life specialists were squirrels in their former life, I'm sure of it! My wife Michelle is a still-life photographer. She has been collecting objects for years. She goes for a weekend in the country and comes home with stuff like an old flaking piece of fencing or a rusted teapot that she knows will look great in a picture she has in mind. In fact, it's probably more accurate to say that the props inspire her to take the picture in the first place. Look for colour and especially for different textures. Of course you may be a collector already.

■ **This shot was based** on a postcard I bought at a gallery. The props are not exactly the same, but I copied the flowing composition that the artist created: everything flows into the next object, from the top tulip down to the bottom petal. I used a big window for lighting and shot on a cheap compact.

If so, start by making a still life with the artefacts you've collected as its theme. Next, consider what you are going to use as a base and background. You then need to collect objects that are sympathetic to, or work well with, the theme and put them all together.

Found still life

Of course, there are potentially wonderful still-life pictures all around us that we just don't see. Still life is as much the art of selection as it is of creation. The ability to select or to find the patterns that exist around us is something we develop during our whole career as photographers.

Sometimes a still life that you shoot on holiday can say more about the country or area you're in than a grand landscape or cityscape. This is because the artefacts in the picture are symbolic of the location.

I love food and I often make a still life of a meal or the café table after a drink and snack. It reminds me later of happy times I enjoyed. There are no rules – just try to develop your critical eye and practise, practise, practise.

■ **Think about colours.** *For this picture I used a bright blue background, from the opposite end of the spectrum to the orange flowers. They fought each other on the page to produce a vibrant colour image.*

223

Considering your viewpoint

BEFORE YOU CAN START MAKING DECISIONS *about your composition you need to set up your camera. A tripod is a must, not only to keep the camera steady and avoid camera shake, but also so that you can keep running back and checking through the viewfinder while you compose the picture.*

Never start composing a still life without the camera set up in position – it will look completely different in the viewfinder.

Once you have set up the camera on the tripod you might think that you can start putting your shot together, but now you have another major consideration – your camera angle. When you slowly move the camera up and down with your eye glued to the viewfinder you will understand why. Camera angle has a dramatic effect on the apparent shape of objects. A bottle viewed from above appears as an entirely different shape to when it is viewed from base level. It's a good learning exercise to shoot the same set-up from several different angles.

■ **These two pictures demonstrate** *how the camera angle can influence the shape of objects in your still life. You can see how the glass appears to be a different shape as the height of camera's viewpoint changes.*

Lenses

The choice of lens is another photographic decision that makes a huge difference to the composition of the picture. As I said in Chapter 12, a wide-angle lens exaggerates perspective. In other words, the objects closer to the lens will appear larger and those further away will appear proportionately smaller than they do to the eye. A wide-angle lens – about 28mm – is often the choice of pros because it allows you to be physically close and to look into the objects.

■ **Altered viewpoints:** *The picture on the left was shot on a 200mm (tele) lens. The branch of the tree appears to be over the basket and the background is out of focus. The picture on the right, shot on a 50mm lens, shows us that the branch is in fact behind the basket. The tele lens has compressed the perspective.*

Conversely, a long-focal-length lens will compress perspective and give the impression that the objects are closer together than they would appear to the eye. The other property of lenses that is important to consider is the depth of focus (or depth of field). The inherent depth of focus of wide-angle lenses means that you will find it easier to hold the subjects sharp from foreground to background.

A lens holds two-thirds of its sharpness past the point of focus and only one-third in front of the point of focus. So focus about one-third of the way into the picture for maximum depth of focus.

Of course you may wish to keep one subject sharp and leave the foreground and/or background in *soft focus*. Or you may choose to use a long (telephoto) lens for its lack of depth of focus. A 28–105mm (or similar) lens is very useful for still life because you can look at wide-angle and long-lens effects without changing lenses.

> **DEFINITION**
>
> **Soft focus,** in this case, means out of focus, giving a soft edge to the subjects.

If you are using a point-and-shoot, remember that you will get greater depth of focus from front to back on the wide-angle setting.

Choice of film

The final major choice is that of film. You can use a slow film (25–100 ISO) for the ultimate in sharpness and fine grain. Or you can go for a fast film (800–3200 ISO), which will give you a grainier, softer result. This can give you a lovely painterly, almost Impressionist feel.

Sometimes I breathe on the lens to give the picture a foggy look in addition to the grain of the film. This can look great.

Most professional still-life photography is shot on large format (5 x 4- or 10 x 8-inch) cameras, because they are the ultimate when it comes to the smooth, sharp reproductions of a subject.

Composition

WHEN YOU START COMPOSING *your still-life pictures, I recommend you begin by just placing objects together in a rather random way – to see if they will work together.*

When you are putting the props together on the background try to see them not as what they are but simply as coloured shapes of various sizes and volumes. That will help you with the composition.

Once you are happy that the colours and shapes work well together, set about building the picture around one dominant object. This is what I do, and as I add each prop I make sure that it relates comfortably to the others. The purpose of this exercise is to combine all the individual objects together to form an aesthetically pleasing whole.

Learn to look carefully at negative space. This is the space between objects that leads the eye from one item to another and connects the objects to form one composition.

■ **This composition** *was based on a simple figure-of-eight. The bright colours of the fruit against the green background have created a wonderful summery feel.*

Choosing a background

When you are satisfied that you have a harmonious group of props, it's time to make a decision on the background. Do you want to go all minimalist and use a white or plain-coloured background that will focus the viewer's eye completely on the props? Or do you want a "real-life" look, using a table as a base and maybe wallpaper for the background? Or a window, or a peeling painted wall?

While we're on the subject of composition, you must, of course, make a decision on whether to shoot a vertical, horizontal, or panoramic composition. That's a very personal decision; some of us see things vertically and some horizontally. I will leave that choice to you, but do think about it.

INTERNET

www.amateurphoto.
about.com/hobbies/
amateurphoto/library/
weekly/aa030498.htm

Check out this web page for some great still-life tips.

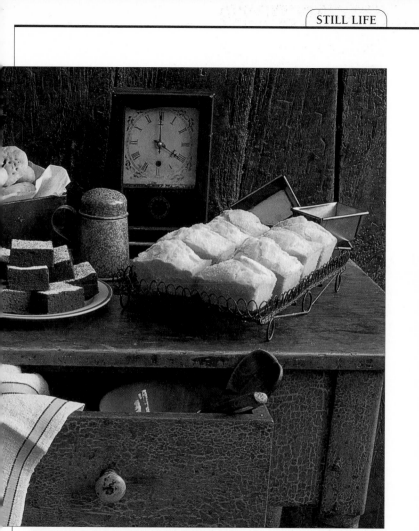

■ **I rescued the background** *for this shot from a rubbish tip, and the props were borrowed from my wife's prop cupboard. I started with the clock and began adding the other bits and pieces, making sure that the negative spaces between the props made harmonious shapes.*

Light and colour

MOST OF THE LIGHTING EFFECTS *that professionals use are based on reproducing window light, so why not go straight to that source? Set up next to the window for sidelight, in front of it for a back-lit picture, or adjacent to it for a cross-light effect.*

Important accessories to window light are reflectors and a large sheet of diffusing material, such as tissue paper, tracing paper, or fibreglass sheeting. You can buy these items from most professional photographic stores. You can change the colour of the light with your reflectors and diffusers. For example, you can use gold reflectors and a pale yellow diffuser (net curtains are good) to reproduce a golden sunset light. In fact, you can manipulate the colours any way you want with reflectors and diffusers of various hues. You can also set up formal still-life pictures outside in the garden using daylight.

When shooting daylight still-life pictures, fit wheels (with brakes!) to the legs of your still-life table base. That way, you can move the setting around to the lighting effect you desire. This is what many pros do.

■ **As the sole light source** *for this photograph, I used the window that you see in the shot at a three-quarters angle, and combined that with a white reflector opposite the window to fill in the shadows. You will be amazed at how effective reflectors can be in still lifes.*

■ **Still life on an old fishing boat in the Loire:** *To soften the light I used a large diffuser, which you can buy cheaply from any big camera store, plus a gold reflector below and in front of the camera to warm the light.*

BOX OF TRICKS

All still-life photographers have their box (usually a DIY toolbox) of essential items that they just can't do without. This is my list of essentials.

- Surgical gloves for handling items without leaving fingerprints
- Tweezers for removing annoying little items like hairs and fluff
- Coloured spray paints for making your own backgrounds
- Scissors
- Permanent-ink pens for retouching marks on objects (scratches, for example)
- Blu-Tack® for holding things in place (especially round objects)
- Dulling spray for removing fierce highlights from shiny surfaces
- A make-up brush for removing crumbs and the like
- Paper towels for mopping up spillage
- Rods for hanging things from
- A fine water spray for putting dew on flowers or condensation on bottles and glasses
- Gaffa tape, because it is very strong and can be reused for many jobs
- Double-sided tape for sticking things together
- A powerful staple gun for fastening backgrounds in place

Black-and-white still life

Still life is a great theme for teaching yourself about black-and-white photography and learning to see colours in terms of tones of grey. You will soon discover what densities of grey various colours convert to. By shooting a multicoloured still life in both colour and black-and-white, you'll get a great start in learning to see in tones.

■ **I was attracted** to the repetition of the curved shapes of this bread display in a midwestern US restaurant. I moved it all a bit closer together to condense the composition, then I used a tripod. The light, from a skylight above, was low but of a beautiful quality, and I knew the picture would look great in black-and-white.

■ **The tones of grey** in this shot of the remains of a meal I had in Tuscany are very different to those in the picture above. I rested my camera on the back of a chair and shot on a compact with a 32mm lens and the flash off.

A word to the wise

IT'S IMPORTANT TO REMEMBER that you will have disappointments shooting still lifes just as in any creative endeavour. You'll have pictures that don't work as well as you had hoped and envisioned. The reason for the disappointment will almost always be that you didn't notice something glaringly ugly – a small, black hair in a glass of milk, for example – that has appeared as if from nowhere in your picture.

Trivia...

I once spent a day (and lots of film) taking a still life for a new fizzy-drink advert. The result was great – apart from the fingerprint on the side of the glass that I hadn't seen!

In still life more than in any other area of photography we have to eliminate the ugly before we can be left with the beautiful. But don't give up, with practice you will improve very quickly.

A simple summary

✓ Don't worry about inspiration – borrow some ideas from your favourite still-life paintings.

✓ If you intend to shoot a lot of still lifes, consider collecting props for use in your pictures.

✓ Be alert to the possibility of still-life studies around you. Why go to the trouble of creating what you could find elsewhere?

✓ Different viewpoints will alter the apparent shapes of objects.

✓ Lenses and film type can have a marked impact on your work. Try as many as you can.

✓ For the purposes of composition it's useful to see things solely in terms of shape and colour.

✓ Window light is the classic choice for still lifes, and it's more adaptable than you might think.

✓ Shooting black-and-white still lifes is a great way to teach yourself how to see in shades of grey.

Chapter 18

Children

THE BIRTH OF ONE'S FIRST CHILD often sparks off the beginning of a person's serious interest in photography. People usually buy their first good camera in the hope of taking better pictures of their children. I had been a professional photographer for some years by the time my first son was born, but Nick's arrival certainly ignited my interest in photographing children. I kept a loaded camera at hand constantly for about 12 years. I shot mostly in black-and-white and the intimacy of this long-term project was a far cry from my photojournalism work of the time.

In this chapter...
- ✓ *Births and beginnings*
- ✓ *Babies and toddlers*
- ✓ *The world of the child*
- ✓ *Kiddie portraits*

Births and beginnings

I BEGAN THE PHOTOGRAPHY *of my own children right at the start:
I was present at the birth of our first son Nick. I had popped a little point-
and-shoot camera in my pocket just in case I didn't pass out and was in a fit
condition to take a picture. The hospital staff said it would be okay and my wife
Michelle said something like, "A photograph is the last of my problems – I don't
care if you shoot* Gone With the Wind *in here right now!" I waited, however,
and supported, and did all the "new man" stuff, and, finally, I took the picture
below about 2 minutes after the birth.*

Before you start shooting, you
must get hospital permission,
and, of course, you must
keep out of the way. A flash
would be intrusive, so this is
the ideal time to use a very
fast film, like a 3200 ISO
black-and-white or a 1600
ISO colour.

If you are using a point-and-
shoot, remember that your
wide-angle has a larger
aperture than the telephoto
and so will enable you to
shoot better in available
light. That moment of the
birth of your child is a
magical one – try to
get a photo of it.

■ **I attended Nick's birth** *with a point-and-shoot in my
pocket, loaded with 1600 ISO black-and-white film, not knowing
whether any of us would be up for a picture. This is now a
favourite family picture and I'm glad I had the camera with me.*

Don't shoot just the firstborn

I also took pictures of Matt's (my second son's) birth, but the one we love most is the
one shown on the opposite page of the two brothers meeting in the hospital for the first
time. It's a situation that one can anticipate will make a great picture because it is a big
family moment – and memories are made of moments like this.

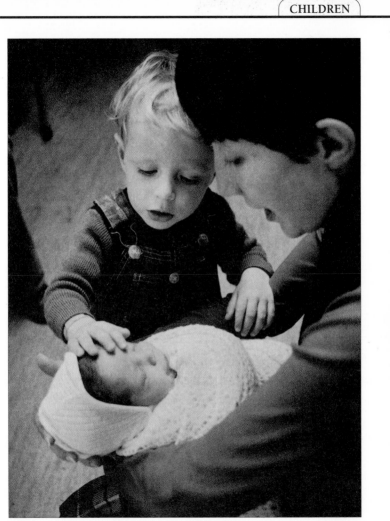

■ **The key to this picture** *was anticipation: I knew Nick would be fascinated by baby Matt. I had my camera loaded with 1600 ISO film and used a large-aperture lens (35mm, f1.4). The slightly wide-angle lens let me get close and intimate. Flash would have killed the mood.*

Babies and toddlers

PHOTOGRAPHING *young babies is not difficult from a logistical point of view. They're pretty easy to photograph because they are not yet on the move. Indeed, it's the only time your kids won't run away or tell you to buzz off (or worse). I am fascinated by their tiny hands, feet, and ears and have taken lots of close-ups.*

I don't feel too comfortable about firing flashes into their faces so I don't use a flash; I do, however, always ensure I have another important piece of equipment – the dribble cloth! They always decide to regurgitate some milk just when you begin shooting. And once you start shooting you must be prepared to take lots of pictures. You might then catch one of those great smiles that paediatricians tell us are caused by wind – no way!

■ **For this picture**, *mother and baby were sat in the window. I shot with a 105mm lens, concentrating on the composition. I love the hand position.*

Working around the baby

As babies start to get on the move, photography becomes a two-person job – they move so fast and safety must come first. Make sure the studio (probably the sitting room) is warm. If the baby is yours you will know when he or she is at his or her best. Is it after a nap? After a meal? If the baby is not your own, ask the parents these details and plan the shoot accordingly. You can't fit baby pictures into your schedule, you must fit into the baby's schedule.

Lighting the scene

I always prefer to utilize the natural light coming through the window, and I recommend you do the same. I use a white reflector opposite the window to bounce the light back towards the baby. You will also need a tripod because using a flash would kill the quality of the window light. Use 800–1600 ISO colour film or 1600–3200 ISO black-and-white film.

When babies are at the pre-walk stage, they are always on the go. If you can't yet direct them to keep still long enough to grab a sharp picture this has to be the flash period.

The flash will freeze the moment and you can catch those great action pictures. If you shoot on an SLR camera, bounce the flash off the ceiling or wall. Or, better still, use a large white card or sheet – 1 x 1.2 metres (3 x 4 ft) is good – and you will soften the lighting. Most 35mm systems include a dedicated flash and I highly recommend you purchase such a system because it enables you to produce perfectly exposed bounced flash or fill-in flash every time. It's worth the investment.

Even with a flash I would recommend fast film (at least 800 ISO) because it requires less flash power, so the batteries last longer and, very importantly, the flash recharges more quickly.

The world of the child

NOW WE REALLY WANT TO take a peek into the world of the child. This is the area of child photography where most of the great pictures come from. When it comes to photographing kids doing their own thing you need to have your priorities right. I used to "stage manage" situations in which children would be really involved and interested: I would take them out to their favourite places or organize games with their friends in the park. And I didn't touch a camera until they were having a good time. Once they started having fun, that's when I got out the camera and started taking pictures.

■ **This picture** *was taken during the magic show at Matt's birthday party. I lay on the floor to capture the kids' faces. They were absorbed with the magician and not interested in me at all – perfect!*

239

My children and their friends became used to me with camera in hand. Photography was a part of our family life and the children just went on with their lives unselfconsciously. There were, of course, many moments along the way when I had to put the camera down because photographs would have been intrusive or an abuse of their trust.

My photography of children became a professional endeavour after people saw my personal pictures. As a professional child photographer I began using models, but I remained convinced that, regardless of whose kids they were, my "good parenting" techniques were just as important as the purely photographic ones in this situation.

Always be prepared

When you are on a day out with the family and the thought of an SLR and zoom just seems too much, pop the point-and-shoot in your pocket. Children have a habit of creating wonderful photo opportunities when you don't have a camera handy and it's those moments that you will most want to capture. Having your point-and-shoot loaded with film and fresh batteries means you have a chance to get those shots. If you find you are not close enough ask your lab if they can make a special reframed print by hand and enlarge the action in the print. When you are using a point-and-shoot, the pre-focus, or focus-lock, technique is going to be very important (see Chapter 6).

■ **Matt had just** *been told to come in and wash for lunch (for the tenth time). I was standing by and snapped his expression. It always pays to keep a loaded camera handy.*

Avoiding red eyes

When shooting kids I recommend that you do not use the red-eye reduction mode on your point-and-shoot.

The delay, created by red-eye reduction modes, between pushing the button and the shutter going off is hopeless for kids' portraits – the expression you loved when you pushed the button is gone by the time the shutter goes.

Use a red-eye reduction pen instead. They are effective and easy to use. In my opinion, red-eye reduction modes are a joke – I've never found one that works!

Make it Natural

I reckon the bottom line is don't make photography a big deal or give it great importance. Try to keep it as a normal part of family life. Pros also need to keep that same relaxed atmosphere in their work.

Never create a bad family tension over a photograph. If the child doesn't want a picture taken then and there you need to respect their wishes. There will always be another opportunity.

My favourite equipment combination is an SLR camera with an 80–200mm zoom. The zoom is ideal because you can compose without having to move. Things can happen so fast you don't have time to move anyway. I use a fast film – 800 ISO colour or 1600 ISO black-and-white – so that I can cope with most light conditions. Exceptions to this would be while on the beach or in similar consistently bright conditions. Then I use 100 or 200 ISO colour or 25 ISO black-and-white film.

■ **These shots were taken** in Vienna, a city that is famous for its pastries (among other things). Matt was in heaven – so I just let the motor drive run. I love motor sequences of children.

Kiddie portraits

ALTHOUGH THERE IS A WHOLE CHAPTER on portraits elsewhere in this book, there are some special considerations you need to bear in mind when making portraits of children.

Quite high on the list of priorities must be to pick a location that is not going to make it difficult to keep the kids focused on the job at hand.

A distraction-free zone

The studio is the only opportunity we have of photographing children without any background distractions. When I say studio I don't mean a formal high-street establishment full of lights and props but rather a set-up with a plain background. Outside against a white wall would be great, or on a balcony or in a conservatory – basically any location with plenty of light. I often spray large sheets of hardboard or plywood and use those as a background, but a bedsheet is great too. I get my tripod and set the camera at the child's eye level. Too many pictures of children are shot from the adult's-eye level, looking down on the child. It is more powerful – and, in fact, more dignified – to be at child level.

If you are shooting just head and shoulders, don't use a wide-angle because you will distort the face, ending up with an elongated head and big nose. Instead, use the tele setting on your compact or a tele on your SLR (70mm or longer is fine). If you only have a fixed-focal-length compact or wide to normal lenses for your SLR, shoot from the waist up to avoid distortion.

Kids should be kids

Children have a short attention span so be prepared before you bring them in front of the camera. Play some of their favourite music. You need to commit yourself to the task, so learn to be an entertainer as well as a photographer. Don't scrub off all their personality for the shoot, let them come as children – relaxed and charming.

The mood of the child will reflect your mood, and he or she will pick up on any tension you are feeling.

If you are photographing children other than your own, I would advise that you ask their parents to keep out of the way. This way you can develop your own relationship with the kids without them looking to a "higher power" for approval.

For some reason many photographers start talking kiddie talk when they are shooting kids. Don't insult them. Give clear, firm instructions: they are small people, not Martians.

If it's not possible to create a daylight studio environment, bounce flash (for SLR users) is a very sympathetic light source. If circumstances demand that you need to use the built-in flash, that will be fine also, but you will probably need to use a red-eye retouch pen later. And why not try using black-and-white film instead? If you are considering creating your own lighting, have another look at Chapter 11.

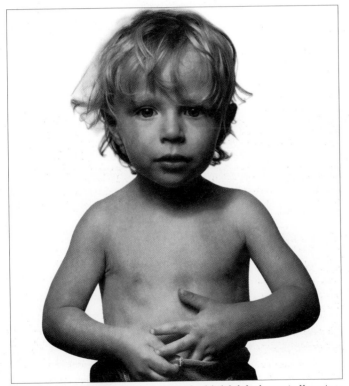

■ **For this shot** of Nick I set up the white background and the light before he came in. He was in the middle of getting ready for bed, and I wanted to capture his tousled, natural look.

Informal, or snapshot, portraits

There is no technical advice to give you here; it's all general. Great snapped portrait opportunities can pop up everywhere – around the house, on the beach, at the shopping precinct – you just need to be alive to the potential. As I have said before, keep your camera handy and capture the natural charm of the child. Most of my best informal portraits have been made when I have observed the children for some time and have framed and focused on them before attracting their attention. It is often one frame and they're off.

■ **This is a good example** *of a child who is happy in his surroundings. I used an 80–200mm zoom – such a useful lens for child photography – set at about 150mm.*

■ **These two little boys** *were too deeply absorbed to notice me. I was attracted to the protective circular shape they had formed. I shot this on an 80–200mm zoom set at 150mm and used a large aperture (f4) to throw the background out of focus.*

Group portraits

From time to time we all have to take a group portrait (of the school football team or whatever). Not easy. First of all you have to take twice as many pictures as you think you need. There is so often a kid with his or her eyes shut... or worse!

Use a tripod so you can keep your hands free to "conduct the orchestra" as it were.

You need to be quite tough here. Be in charge, place every child exactly where you want them. Take no nonsense. You need a good idea of the composition you want before you shoot.

The kids must be able to see the camera out of both eyes, so tell them to shut each eye in turn to make sure they can. I'm afraid there is no escape: you are the one on show, and you need to throw yourself into the entertainer role. But making a complete ass of yourself can be very worthwhile in the end. Really any lens will be fine – just get all those kids looking good.

■ **During this class portrait session,** *one kid started the binocular look and, surprise surprise, they all wanted to do it! I just snapped away. Note the low camera angle, so they are looking straight at me.*

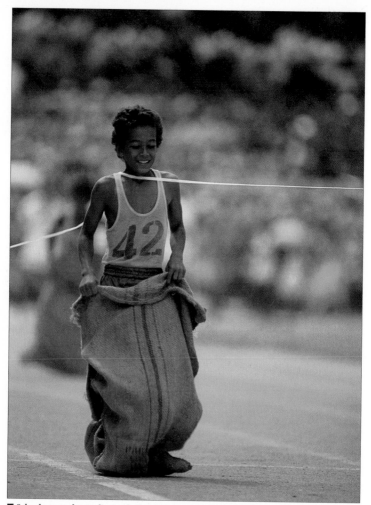

■ **School sports day in the Seychelles:** *I pre-focused on the finishing line, easily predicting the winner's joyful expression. Don't just snap away – think about it. The best ad lib is a rehearsed ad lib.*

Events

Whether it's a christening or a sports day, the most important consideration is the programme of the event. Talk to the person in charge to find out exactly what's going to happen and where and when you should position yourself for the highlights of the event. You can't chase an event because you will find yourself constantly scrambling to grab pictures. Also you will inevitably be a pain in the butt to everybody else by excusing yourself and trying to get into good camera positions.

When photographing events, always ensure you have plenty of shots left on the roll and a new roll ready in your pocket.

I would say that photographing children, especially my own, has given me more pleasure than any other area of photography. I feel creating pictures of your children that will become cherished by the whole family should be a part of family life, and the camera should be as familiar as the telephone or TV.

A simple summary

✓ If you want photographic records of your kids, start at the beginning – the births – and make the camera a normal part of your life.

✓ Do your bit to deter sibling rivalry: if you photograph one birth, photograph them all!

✓ No matter whose toddler you're taking pictures of, you will have to adapt to the kid's schedule.

✓ If possible use natural lighting for photographing children.

✓ No matter where you go with your own kids, make sure you've got some sort of camera to hand – you'll regret it otherwise.

✓ Don't miss a great shot waiting for the red-eye reduction to kick in – retouch the picture later.

✓ Let the child act like a child. Get the parents out of the way and have some fun!

✓ When shooting group portraits be sure to turn on the charm. It's the only way to get great shots.

✓ Don't follow the action of sports days and the like. Set yourself up and let the action come to you.

Chapter 19

Action

WE'VE ALL BEEN knocked out by some of the great sports photographs that appear in the press. There's no way the average person can produce images like those. Most sports photographers are specialists – they don't do anything else. Their equipment is hugely expensive, they have unique access, and they plan some pictures for months. However, not all action is sports action; catching the look between two people in a restaurant is as important an action picture as a shot from the World Cup. You can take terrific action shots simply through knowledge of your equipment, good planning, and concentration.

In this chapter...

✓ Interpreting action

✓ Getting an angle on the action

✓ The advantage of autofocus

✓ Point-and-shoot action

EVEN SUBTLE ACTION SHOTS CAN BE DRAMATIC

Interpreting action

EVERYONE LOVES A GOOD ACTION SHOT. *Whether it's a close-up of the knockout punch in a boxing match or a goalkeeper making a vital save, or indeed something less dramatic, like someone making a mad dash for shelter in a sudden rainstorm, a good action picture lets you really feel what the subject of the photo is going through.*

The first thing you should know is that there are several basic ways in which we can photograph action, each of which results in a different effect.

1 Keep the camera still and use either a fast shutter speed or a flash. This gives the effect of freezing the action.

■ **I have frozen** *Matt's jump with flash in this picture. You can see every detail of the action. If there had been more light I could have frozen the action with a fast shutter speed instead.*

2 Use a slower shutter speed (between ¹⁄₃₀ and ¹⁄₆₀ of a second) and pan the camera with the action going past you. This results in the moving object being sharp because you moved the camera at the same speed as the object, keeping it in the middle of the viewfinder, while the background will be streaked, giving the impression of speed.

■ **This time I panned** *with Matt as he ran past me. To give a good feeling of speed I used a shutter speed of ¹⁄₃₀ of a second. The combination of the fast shutter speed and the pan has had the effect of leaving the face recognizable while blurring everything else.*

3 Shoot on an even slower shutter speed (¼ of a second) and allow everything to move – the action, the camera, yourself – everything. You end up with a semi-abstract picture of blurred movement, which can look stunning in colour. Ernst Haas used this technique way back in the 1950s for his magnificent series on bullfighting and rodeos.

■ **This time** *I went all the way and used a ¼-of-a-second shutter speed on this pan. Everything is blurred. I love the swirling shapes. Try it in colour – it can look really great.*

4 Combine the use of flash with a slow shutter speed. The slow shutter speed blurs everything and the flash freezes the movement to make a blurred picture with a frozen central image. The latest dedicated flashguns allow you to set the flash to fire at the end of the shutter movement so you get the movement behind the action image. This results in a very pleasing effect.

■ **There is a combination** *of flash and daylight in this shot. The flash has frozen the main action, but the ¹/₃₀-of-a-second shutter speed is slow enough to add some blur for a different interpretation of movement.*

Don't punch the shutter button in the heat of the moment, no matter how tempting it seems. A punch will jerk the camera and the result will be an out-of-focus picture. You need to squeeze it gently.

Getting an angle on the action

AN IMPORTANT CONSIDERATION *of action photography is the angle at which the action is coming to you. This is a key factor in the shutter's ability to freeze the action.*

To illustrate the importance of angle, consider the following. An action of a cyclist going past you would require, say, $\frac{1}{500}$ to $\frac{1}{1000}$ of a second to hold it sharp. However, if the cyclist was coming towards you at the same speed at a three-quarter angle, it would only take $\frac{1}{250}$ of a second to keep it sharp. Furthermore, if he was coming directly at you, it would only require between about $\frac{1}{60}$ and $\frac{1}{125}$ of a second.

Never chase the action. You need to anticipate where it is going to occur. Whether it's the finish line of a track event or the goalmouth at a football match, get there first, be focused, and wait for the action to come to you.

■ **These galloping horses in Morocco** *are sharp even though I only used a shutter speed of $\frac{1}{125}$ of a second because they are travelling towards me.*

You must try to anticipate peak action. If you squeeze the button when a high jumper is at that moment at the top of his leap, when for a split second he is not going up or down, you can freeze action on a slow shutter speed ($\frac{1}{60}$ of a second). There are many examples of this in action pictures taken in the 19th century.

The great saying by sports photographers is "If you see the peak action in your viewfinder, it's too late." You must be pushing the button before the action peaks in order to capture it.

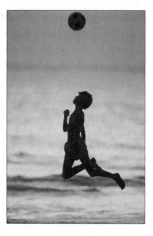

■ **I caught this action** *at about $\frac{1}{60}$ of a second. The boy is at the peak of the action, not going up and not going down. I could have frozen him at $\frac{1}{30}$ of a second.*

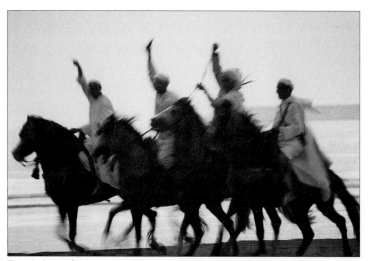

■ **As the horses** *flew past me I was able to capture that feeling – creating a blurring effect – using exactly the same shutter speed of $\frac{1}{125}$ of a second.*

The advantage of autofocus

THE RAPID IMPROVEMENT *in autofocus technology over recent years has been a great bonus for the sports photographer. It has allowed photographers to concentrate on composition and content without having to be anxious about the sharpness of the image. If you set your camera and lens on continuous autofocus and make sure your shutter speed is fast enough to freeze the action, you will be able to take sharp action pictures.*

Motor drives are also useful but don't be fooled into believing that the autofocus and the motor drive combined will take great pictures for you. You still need to plan, anticipate, and compose your shots.

No matter how much cool photography equipment you're lugging around, it is still *you* who has to take the picture. Someone with a point-and-shoot camera and an intimate knowledge of the sport or action subject will produce better pictures than a person with all the gear and no understanding of what they are trying to photograph.

USING A MOTOR DRIVE WITH AUTOFOCUS

The autofocus has made this sort of action sequence a piece of cake. I love making motor-drive sequences when shooting action. A series of action frames taken at a rate of up to 2½ shots per second tells a much different story than a single frame does. This series shows us how well co-ordinated and well balanced little boys can be.

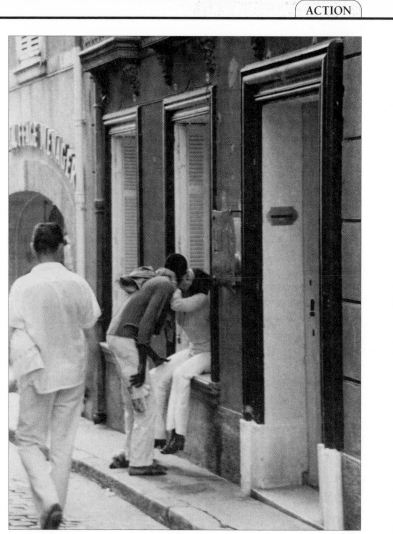

■ **Capturing action** *isn't all about sports, of course. This romantic interlude is about anticipation, too. It's all about grabbing that magic moment.*

Even the smallest movement is an action, and all action photography – and that includes more than just sports photography – always requires anticipation and concentration to capture the moment.

When covering a sports event look for non-action picture opportunities too, such as the anguished loser or the deep concentration of an athlete in preparation.

When I shoot sport I take two SLR bodies, one 35–70mm zoom lens (f2.8 autofocus), one 80–200mm zoom (f2.8 autofocus), one 300mm (f4 autofocus), 400 ISO colour film and both 400 and 1600 ISO black-and-white (depending on the weather), a monopod, a folding stool to sit on, a flask of coffee, and a pen and notebook for captions. Obviously I also have to wear a photographer's waistcoat with lots of reinforced pockets!

I recommend you use a monopod when shooting with long lenses. Telephoto lenses get heavy and a monopod allows you to get the weight off your arms and concentrate on sharp, exciting pictures.

■ **This action has been frozen** by a very fast shutter speed, ¹⁄₂₀₀₀ of a second. The camera has shown us more than the human eye can see. The splashing water has been frozen into a beautiful pattern of droplets. Aren't the possibilities of photography great?

Point-and-shoot action

I CAN'T PRETEND that you have the same potential for shooting great action shots with a point-and-shoot camera as you do with a modern SLR.

Some of the greatest sports pictures are made by remote-control cameras. The photographer sets up a camera position in anticipation of where the action will occur. He or she then fires the shutter (usually with a motor drive in full swing) with an infrared shutter release from up to 200 metres (650 ft) away.

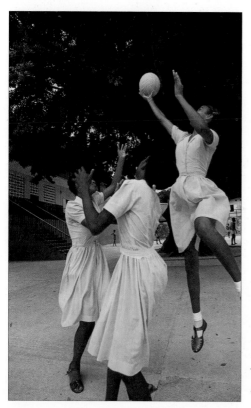

INTERNET

www.geocities.com/click brah/surfphototips.htm

Check out this web page for some useful tips on how to photograph surfing action. There are some great photographs too!

■ **I planned this shot.** *I knew that most of the peak action would be near the hoop, so I camped out there. I pre-focused on the anticipated action area and concentrated on hitting the peak of the action. I missed a few and so will you, but don't worry – you'll get a couple of good shots that'll make all the waiting worthwhile.*

257

I have discussed the point-and-shoot in detail in Part Two, but I think I should go over the specific points again with regards to action photography.

 The shutter speeds of point-and-shoot cameras aren't as fast those on SLRs. In fact, the shutter speed is often relative to the price of the camera. They start at about $\frac{1}{200}$ of a second for a basic model and go up to $\frac{1}{500}$ of a second for an expensive one. However, with most point-and-shoots you won't actually know what the shutter speed is (unless it's a super-compact). But don't worry, we can out-think the machine and still produce some cracking action shots. For example, if you use a fast film, say 800–1600 ISO, and the light is reasonably bright, you will force the camera into shooting on its fastest shutter speed. If you want to go for a panned or really blurred arty movement picture, you can force the camera to use a slow shutter speed by loading slow film (100 ISO).

■ **To capture this moment** *I pre-focused on the bank with my point-and-shoot and waited for the child to jump. There is a little blur, but I don't mind that.*

 The autofocus is much slower on a point-and-shoot camera.

Autofocus lenses designed for top-of-the-range SLR cameras have a built-in motor that drives the autofocus — they can now follow and stay focused on most moving objects.

The telephoto facility is much shorter in focal length and the maximum aperture much smaller than on an SLR camera. At 115mm telephoto setting the maximum aperture of a point-and-shoot is about f10. On the other hand, SLR telephoto lenses of as long as 300mm can have a maximum aperture of f2.8. That means that the lens will let in eight times as much light on to the film and allow you to use a faster shutter speed to obtain correct exposures.

You can offset the slow autofocus system of a point-and-shoot to some extent by practising the focus-lock, or pre-focus, technique described in Chapter 6. This way, you will still be able to create some great action pictures.

■ **Look for the unusual** *angles on action. I was in the pool with my underwater camera when Matt jumped over the top of me. I love that crazy angle!*

A simple summary

✓ Regardless of what action you are shooting, you should be trying to capture the spirit or feeling of the moment.

✓ There are basic ways to capture action, each of which gives a different result.

✓ You will get a totally different picture by shooting something moving past you than you will shooting the same subject moving towards you at the same speed.

✓ The best action shots are those that show the peak action. You must learn to anticipate peak action in order to capture it.

✓ Autofocus and motor drives are great... but they can't take a great picture for you.

✓ Point-and-shoot cameras have certain shortcomings when it comes to photographing action. However, it is still possible to get really good results if you know how to override the system.

Chapter 20

Travel

TRAVEL PHOTOGRAPHY embraces almost the whole range of classic photographic themes: travelling photographers make portraits, landscapes, still lifes, and architectural pictures. However, I think travel photography requires its own chapter because of the special circumstances in which you'll have to take your pictures.

In this chapter...

✓ What is travel photography?
✓ The travel photographer
✓ Thinking equipment
✓ Land-based travel pics
✓ Extra tips for the land based
✓ Underwater and the beach
✓ Travel themes and obsessions

THE SECRET TO BEAUTIFUL TRAVEL SHOTS IS MAKING SURE YOU'RE NOT ALL AT SEA

What is travel photography?

FOR MOST OF US, *travel photography means holiday photography. In the real world that carries the baggage of logistical problems such as not enough time, terrible weather, kids fighting in the back of the car, a bored partner desperate to get back to the hotel in time for happy hour, scaffolding all over your favourite building, a tummy upset, sunburnt shoulders... I could go on forever! Having taken pictures in more than 75 countries I have encountered them all. But am I bitter? No!*

Okay, so travel and taking photographs – not just snapshots but satisfying pictures that will evoke great memories for years – is a hassle. But most of the hassle is caused by the normal everyday stress of travelling. This chapter deals with the techniques of successful travel as much as it does with photographic technique, discussing the logistics of travelling as much as the actual taking of the photographs. This is all important stuff because, after all, it's people who take pictures, not cameras.

■ **Matt was happy** *to be photographed at the beach because he thought he looked cool. I shot this with an underwater point-and-shoot – these cameras are great for holiday snaps.*

The before-leaving-home stuff

Most of us don't just get up in the morning and decide on a whim to go on holiday. So, before going away, there's a whole load of things that we need to do. The following points are, I feel, invaluable.

Research

Great holidays and great travel pictures are the rewards of great planning. Research is the key word. Don't automatically book the package-tour holiday because it's easy and, at first glance, good value. I always find that by booking a flight and then researching the local hotels (the Internet is invaluable for this), I get a better deal than the available packages.

I recently went to Goa in India for a 2-week rest in the sun. Going completely against my own advice (because I was being lazy), I booked a package deal. The hotel was okay, but it was part of a well-known international chain so I knew exactly what to expect. On my second day I found a wonderful Goan family hotel that was very comfortable and had wonderful food. I could have stayed there for a fraction of the price of the big-name hotel.

Making an agenda

These days there are excellent travel guides available to almost anywhere on earth. Whether you are staying in your own country or going abroad, buy some and study them before you set off. Plan the holiday based on photographic potential. What part of the country is the most beautiful at your holiday time of year? Are there festivals going on? Is it too hot, too cold, or just right? Make a list of your criteria.

I would advise against taking the hotel-organized tours when abroad. There's a handful of reasons for my saying that: you can't stop to take pictures when you want to, the tour may only go to the most touristy places, and there will always be too many people around. Do as I do: use a local guide or cab driver and go alone or share the costs and experience with a like-minded individual, couple, or family that you've met at the hotel.

Camera: old or new?

Every time you go on a photography holiday you'll have to make an equipment choice. Well, you won't *have* to, but the chances are you will make a choice: whether to take your old camera (which might not even be that old) or to buy a new one. Either way, there's a couple of points to bear in mind.

Never take a new camera on a trip without first shooting at least two rolls as a test and a "get-to-know-each-other" sort of thing.

Try out all the modes on a new camera. I suggest that you make yourself a list with diagrams of all the modes, as a reminder of what they all do. Otherwise you might forget. I know, because I do. And don't forget to pack the instruction book in your camera bag.

The same advice applies to your old camera. Get it out and check it's working. Shoot a roll and have it processed 2 weeks before you leave, just in case it needs to be repaired or replaced.

■ **Don't go away** *with any camera – new or old – without first making sure it's in good working order.*

Other important bits

A few weeks before you are due to go away, create a checklist of everything you need to do, crossing items off as they are accomplished. Don't forget your travel insurance (and be sure to check the small print). I always pay that bit extra to include the cost of flying home in case of illness or accident (especially with children). And if you are travelling to exotic locations, check the current state of malaria in that part of the world, and order and start taking the correct malaria pills if necessary. The situation is always changing so check it out. I always make sure my tetanus and hepatitis jabs are up to date. You should also check the legal situation in areas you are travelling in. For example, is it illegal to take any pictures of airports, military personnel, and other potentially "sensitive" subjects?

Always make sure you have small bills of the local currency to tip cab drivers and service staff when you arrive.

The travel photographer

MY WIFE AND I TRAVELLED *all over the world with our two sons from babyhood until they were in their late teens, so I have had to develop my diplomatic and negotiating skills over the years. Just because you have a partner (and perhaps children) that doesn't mean that you are no longer enthusiastic about your photography... right?*

However, although the photography may be a very important aspect of your holiday, it's possible that the rest of the family couldn't care less about it. It's very important that photography adds enjoyment to the whole family's holiday and doesn't introduce tension. Sometimes your partner may be more interested in getting back to the hotel in time for happy hour than he or she is in the glorious sunset over the mountain range. So be it, fair enough, give in. "No happy hour" can mean "no happy tomorrow" and a black mark against photography. So bear that in mind.

■ **I shot this stunning** *Art Deco-style Miami Beach hotel on a compact camera with the zoom at 105mm. There was a lot of light so I used 100 ISO film for sharpness, fine grain, and colour saturation.*

Getting "that shot" while keeping the family happy

I have often noticed a potential masterpiece in the late afternoon while driving towards the hotel. In such cases, I jump out and very quickly take a compass reading and then drive on. If by early morning the light is potentially interesting, I go out early, take a shot, and then rejoin the family in time for breakfast. I have my "masterpiece" and the family is content. Perfect.

Cars and children

When travelling by car with your kids, don't be too ambitious: you will never get as far each day as you think. Start looking for a hotel or motel by 4 p.m. That tension of finding accommodation when everybody is tired and grumpy can be very uncomfortable. In fact, take pillows and blankets so the kids can have a siesta on the way. Since we had boys we always took a football so they could let off some steam at every stop. Once you get settled in at the hotel, maybe the kids can have a swim while you go out and take a nice sunset shot.

■ **Dawn in the Masai Mara** (Kenya) – with the family fast asleep, I went out with the camp guide John, made some pictures (300mm lens, 800 ISO film), and got back for breakfast.

I find that any sort of physical discomfort or general stress from things going wrong distracts me from my photographic quest. So I now know that I ignore my personal needs at my peril or, at least, the detriment of my photography.

Rather than being an obstacle to me taking pictures I found that the children added to my travel photography. Many of my favourite holiday pictures are those of the boys. They were always enthusiastic about running up a big sand hill or climbing rocks to give me the scene I needed. Children also open up photo opportunities because they make contact with people or stimulate an introduction that proves productive. When in Kenya years ago, my son Nick (who was 6 at the time) used to love playing with African children and was fascinated by their home-made toys. He broke down barriers and we would soon find ourselves laughing and chatting (usually in sign language) with the parents, who normally had very little contact with white people. And the sympathetic atmosphere always led to photographs.

Nick became interested in graffiti and hip-hop culture at about 13 years old and started taking pictures of graffiti wherever he went; so he became a travel photographer too.

If your whole family is interested in photography, all is well and good, but, if no one but you is, you have a couple of courses of action:

 Visit picturesque places that the whole family will be interested in

 Go off and take pictures by yourself and leave the family and/or partner to get on with their holiday

■ **This Masai girl** *had become friendly with Nick, and once she had relaxed, she let me take a picture. The light was very hard, but I shot this photograph under a tree in lovely, shaded light. Having kids with you can be a barrier breaker. They are oblivious to racial tensions.*

I usually planned half a day for pictures and half a day for family – although family times often produced the best pictures.

Women travellers

Research the culture of the country you're visiting with regards to the woman's role, and act appropriately. Cover up in Muslim countries, for instance, otherwise you will attract unwanted attention, both as a woman and as a photographer. Don't take a handbag out with you – too easy for thieves; wear trousers and jackets with secure pockets.

Keep equipment light – it seems to get heavier as the day gets longer. Take a phrase book and don't drink too much, since women's toilets are often few and far between. Don't buy gifts on the way (this applies to men, too) – carrying them is a real pain while you are shooting. Instead, set aside separate shopping days.

Always carry a mobile phone, and note the address and telephone number of your hotel before you leave for the day.

Be VERY wary of offers by men to be your guide. Do your research and know where you are going. As a woman you can often communicate more easily in foreign climes. My wife Michelle made some fine pictures of a harem of Muslim women preparing for a wedding in Marrakech. I would never have been allowed to get near such a situation. A light monopod is great for when you need to take a longish exposure. It also serves as a walking stick and as a defensive weapon.

Thinking equipment

NOW WE GET DOWN to that big question: what equipment do I take? At the bottom of this page you'll find a suggested list for the point-and-shoot photographer. Turn the page for my list of suggestions for the advanced SLR or rangefinder 35mm photographers.

One thing I would advise is that you take your film with you rather than buying it at your destination. Even if you are visiting a city in the summer you will often find you are shooting on the shady side of the street or indoors, so 400 ISO film should be standard.

I recommend you take 20- or 24-exposure films rather than 36-exposure films because it means you can load fast film of 1000 or 1600 ISO into your camera for very-low-light situations, like restaurants, and not be stuck with too many unused exposures.

SPARE FILM: ESSENTIAL EQUIPMENT

COMPACT LIST

This is my suggested equipment list for point-and-shoot users:

1. A 28mm fixed-focal-length compact – they are small and you can "get more in" because they have a wide-angle lens

2. A 35–100mm zoom compact or similar (32–85mm or 36–115mm, for example) for the versatility and the telephoto facility

3. A few throwaway, single-use compacts – just in case

ZOOM COMPACT

Advanced List

The following list is what I take with me:

1. Two 35mm SLR bodies

2. A 28–70mm f2.8 zoom – a good all-round workhorse of a lens

3. An 80–200mm f2.8 zoom – a great lens taking me from long focal length to tele

4. A 300mm f4+1.4 tele converter – I use this when I want to compress perspective, but if I don't carry it around, I use it for working from the car

5. An 18mm very-wide-angle lens for city panoramas or interiors, or if I want to exaggerate the perspective for graphic effect (see Chapter 12)

6. A 28mm PC (perspective-control) lens – I take this if I am planning to shoot architectural pictures, which I usually do

7. A 50mm f1.4 lens – a lens with a very large aperture, which allows me to shoot in low light without resorting to flash

8. A dedicated flashgun, which I use only in emergencies or for special effects

9. A 28mm fixed-focal-length compact camera, which I will slip into my pocket for when I really can't be bothered to take all the other gear but would hate myself if I missed out on a good picture

As well as all that, I carry the following accessories:

- A polarizing filter
- A red filter
- A yellow filter
- Spare batteries (I install new batteries at home before travelling, too)
- A compass
- A torch in case of emergencies or the need to add some light to a still-life picture
- A compact tripod that fits easily into my suitcase
- A space blanket folds into nothing, makes a fine reflector, and is also comforting to have for emergencies

Packing worries

As I said earlier, if you're not prepared for the everyday stress of travel, you won't be up to taking good pictures, so there are certain items that are must-haves on holiday.

Essentials for me are:

- Guide books
- Maps
- A compass
- A good novel
- Swiss Army knife
- Plastic bags
- Elastic bands
- A mobile phone
- A space blanket
- Several pens, including a permanent waterproof marker
- Spare batteries (2 sets)
- Suntan lotion
- Moisturizing cream
- Lip salve
- Sunblock

- A sun hat
- Sunglasses
- Malaria pills, if appropriate
- Sodium chloride tablets for hot weather
- Eye wash
- Painkillers
- Insect repellent
- Insect after-bite lotion
- Underwater goggles and snorkel (I hate hiring much-used ones – urgh!)
- Receipts for all my equipment in case I'm stopped at customs
- Toiletries, of course
- Vitamin tablets

When travelling to both hot and cold locations on the same trip I pack for hot weather and take thermal underwear for cold plus a puffa jacket that will squash up and take up little space. I pack my photographer's waistcoat for all locations.

■ **I find** *my photographer's waistcoat to be absolutely indispensable when travelling. It's got plenty of pockets for spare film, batteries, and all manner of bits that I need to do the job.*

Land-based travel pics

IN THESE PAST FEW CHAPTERS I've covered most of the subjects that
you'll encounter on your travels from both technical and creative points of view.
But here are some tips on other subjects that may interest you – things that are
often quite specific to travel photography.

On safari

Lodges or safari camps? Both can be pricey,
but safari camps in places like the Masai Mara
Game Reserve, in Kenya, are by far the most
enjoyable. You are really out among the
animals à la *Out of Africa* and, although you
sleep in tents, the food is usually excellent and
you are well protected by guards at all times.
Included in the price is a guide and a four-
wheel-drive vehicle at your personal disposal.
This is fantastic for photography. The guides
have a great knowledge of and respect for the
animals and they respond to your enthusiasm.

Instead of a tripod I use a beanbag – three-
quarters full of beans or pebbles – inside a
plastic bag. I lay this over the car's window
ledge and then sit the tele lens on the bag.
This offers great flexibility and support. A
conventional tripod is pretty useless really,
since there is nowhere to set it. Animals are at
their most active early in the morning and late
afternoon, when the light is low, so you need
faster film than you would at first expect.
Using 400–800 ISO should be fine.

■ **Sunset in the Masai Mara** with the whole family on
board. The boys were knocked out by this sight – one that
none of us will ever forget. I used a 400mm lens to "pull
up" the sun, making it appear both larger and closer to
the animals. I supported the lens on a beanbag.

To be honest, it's very unlikely that you will be able to shoot dramatic individual shots of wild animals with a compact camera, but you can take wonderful shots of herds of wildebeest and buffalo, for example. For wildlife photography, a 300mm lens almost becomes the norm. Most wildlife specialists work from 200mm up to 1000mm.

Patience is required by the bagload for safari shoots. The great wildlife photographers plan and track for many days just to get one great shot. It's worse than fishing! Once again, you must research your subject. The more knowledge you have of the animals you are photographing, the more you will be able to anticipate a good shot.

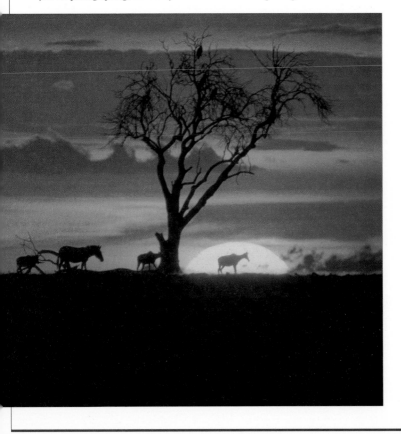

Remember you're not at the movies. These animals – although they're not there waiting to gobble you up – are dangerous.

Never get carried away and go off-road in a normal two-wheel-drive car to photograph a big game animal. It is very dangerous.

At the zoo

Of course, you don't have to go to Africa for great animal shots: you can try the zoo. Although many people are not happy with the idea of zoos, they have improved greatly during recent years.

Have a chat with a gamekeeper to find out the feeding times, and seek advice on which are the star animals – the photogenic ones. The zoom on your compact will usually get you close enough for a good zoo portrait. Remember though that you will still need 800 ISO film because your zoom only has a small aperture.

■ **I took this photograph** *at the zoo. I was able to see the tiger over the fence. I used an 80–200mm zoom set at 200mm and shot at f2.8 to throw the background out of focus and make it seem less like a zoo.*

Landmarks

If you are in a country where you face a language barrier, a useful tip is to buy a set of postcards of all the famous landmarks of the city. You can then show them to cab drivers or friendly locals so they can drive or direct you where you want to go.

You should be able to work out, with your map and compass, when the light will be falling on the buildings or monuments you wish to visit. You can then plan your days to be at each location in the best photographic and viewing light.

Always carry the name, address, and, if possible, a picture of your hotel, then you will (hopefully) never get lost. Taking a bus tour on the first day in a city is good for getting your bearings and you can mark the places of personal interest on your map as you go.

■ **For this dawn shot** *of St Peter's in Rome I found my camera position the day before. It was shot on a 200mm lens and I used a tripod to steady the ¹/₃₀-of-a-second shutter speed.*

Getting the best light

I have often got overexcited on the first day of my holiday and wasted film. With the aid of your compass, calculate what time of day would be best, in terms of light, for the landmarks you wish to photograph.

Don't shoot all your film on the first couple of days. Take it easy at first and you will start to see better pictures as you go along.

Once you have the geography and features of the city in your head and on your map, start working in any local culture, sports, and historic events that interest you. You've already done research on all these at home... haven't you?

Architecture shots

Most specialist architectural photographers use large format (5 x 4-inch) cameras. This is because the larger negative size ensures the ultimate sharpness in the fine details of the building. Also the camera movement enables the photographer to correct perspective. Professional travel photographers mostly use 35mm and correct perspective with a perspective-control (PC) lens. I use a 28mm PC lens.

Light is the magic ingredient in architectural photography. Generally speaking, your research and reconnaissance should tell you at which time of day the light is most sympathetic to your building, since light suits most structures and brings out the detail. If your time is limited, spend 70 per cent of that time looking and 30 per cent shooting. Walk around and find the most dramatic angles. Don't just try to work close up with a wide-angle lens and setting. Move back and take in the whole building in its environment. If your lens will take you close enough, shoot some details too, especially on old buildings.

■ **The Lloyds Building in London,** *which I always felt was a load of factory-like junk! I walked around it till I found the angle that best described my feelings for it, then I shot it on 100 ISO transparency film, using a 20mm lens.*

Because of its fine grain and sharpness, slow film is the preferred choice for architecture, but don't let that get in your way: 400 ISO is fine. When shooting interiors you will mostly need a tripod or monopod. Turn off the flash (if you can't turn it off, put your finger over it) to ensure you capture the lighting and atmosphere that the architect created.

For SLR users, a polarizing filter will increase contrast and produce dramatic dark skies with white clouds in colour. On black-and-white film, a red filter will do the same job.

INTERNET

www.photosecrets.com/ tips.htm

PhotoSecrets is a series of travel guides aimed at photographers. This page of their web site contains a whole load of useful tips.

■ **The dramatic light** *on the building really makes this shot. To exaggerate the perspective I used a 24mm lens and, with the exposure-compensation mode, I shot at -1 stop, resulting in the shadows going almost black.*

Extra tips for the land based

THE FOLLOWING TIPS are things that just wouldn't necessarily have slotted easily into any of the previous pages in this chapter. And although I say they are for land-based photography that's simply because I'm making the assumption that, if you are shooting at the beach or underwater, you will probably not be wearing the sort of clothing that I mention here!

Always take at least two credit cards away with you and ID other than your passport. When you go off rambling around you can leave one card and your passport in the hotel safe with your travellers' cheques, air ticket, and other valuables. Separate your cash.

When you go out taking photos, put enough cash in your sock or bra to get you back to the hotel in case you are pick-pocketed.

Dressing sensibly

It's very important that you wear good walking shoes and a shirt with a collar so that the camera straps don't cut into your neck. Fit wide straps to your cameras for the same reason. A photographer's waistcoat allows me to carry spare film, a notebook and pen, a map, a torch, a Swiss Army knife, a small compass, postcards, and two extra lenses. This means I don't need a camera bag! In cities you will do an awful lot of walking so you must look after your own comfort... and safety. A bush jacket or military jacket is also a good idea – they are strong and have plenty of pockets.

Communicating with the locals

Successful travel photographers are great communicators, especially in places where they don't speak the language. Sympathetic sign and body language plus a smile are important. Don't be afraid to ask the locals for favours, like "Can I shoot a picture of the city from your balcony please?" You will be surprised how co-operative people can be. You are after all showing interest in their city, which they appreciate.

When photographing local people be polite and ask first. Most people say yes, but some will say no (often for religious reasons). Don't mess them around – be ready with your film loaded and camera set up.

In developing countries the question of tipping models comes up. I personally, as a professional, feel it's only fair to pay people who are kind enough to pose for me. Not a lot of money – but it can be their only source of income. Fair enough. You must do what you feel is the right thing.

Underwater and the beach

THE UNDERWATER WORLD is indeed fantastic and a rich subject for photography. But the sheer wonder of it can induce such an adrenaline rush that it's easy to get carried away, and that can be very dangerous. Safety is more important than photographs.

For the novices among us – by that I mean those who are snorkelling for the first time – be sure to wear a shirt or waterproof block-out sun cream. Sunburn can be severe when snorkelling close to the surface.

If scuba diving is more your thing – and you are experienced – you should be well versed in safety procedures. However, the added excitement of taking pictures means you need to be even more disciplined than usual. Never dive with a company that does not ask for your licence first, and be sure to check their equipment. If you're not an experienced diver and are travelling to a great reef location take a course before you go. Although many famous dive resorts offer courses by excellent instructors, it cuts into your photography schedule. Even when snorkelling, don't go it alone – have a diving partner. Personally, I don't dive even in the tropics without a wet suit: I don't like coral cuts or sunburn.

Never get carried away with the picture potential and dive alone or leave your diving partner.

■ **This picture was shot** with an underwater camera on Australia's *Great Barrier Reef. Note that the colour is greenish. I could have corrected that with either a red filter or by using flash, but I liked it as it was.*

Trivia...
Some years ago I was taking some underwater pictures while snorkelling in Cancún, Mexico. I got so carried away that the sea swell made me very seasick. I won't go into detail, but it wasn't a pretty sight!

INTERNET

www.fodors.com/focus

This web page, "How to Take Travel Pictures Like a Pro", gives some great hints and tips for all manner of travel photography. It's definitely worth having a look at.

You can take wonderful underwater pictures with underwater point-and-shoot cameras. They have a built-in flash, and that's great because it puts back the colour that the water filters out, like the reds and yellows. Around midday is the best time for underwater photography because the sun is directly overhead and gets maximum penetration through the water surface. Early and late in the day the sunlight bounces off the water at an angle and you lose a lot of light.

Underwater cameras are also ideal for beach photography since they are impervious to sand and salt water. You can sit them on the beach, wash them off in the water later, and then keep shooting.

■ **This is one of my favourite** *holiday pictures of my son Nick. It was shot on a compact underwater camera in the hotel swimming pool. I sat on the bottom of the pool wearing a weight belt and using a long snorkel. You really must wear goggles for underwater shots or else you can't see through the viewfinder.*

Go as close to your subjects as possible, because everything looks closer underwater than it really is. Also the flash will bounce off small particles of algae and the like floating in the water, upsetting your exposure.

Colour balance

The biggest problem with underwater photography is colour balance. The water filters out the colours at the warm end of the spectrum, and the deeper you dive, the more blue-green the colour cast becomes, and exposure becomes more of a problem. Flash becomes essential for capturing the reds and oranges of some reef fish. By using print film you can improve the colour balance later in the printing stage (or, rather, your minilab can) – although I do love that underwater cast sometimes.

Underwater cameras

There are several excellent underwater housings that you can fit your standard SLR into, but they are expensive and I would suggest that you go looking for a second-hand underwater camera instead. They are tough and last forever.

If you are taking your good camera to the beach, you need a waterproof, sandproof bag. Also, some film manufacturers sell great plastic zip-up film bags.

If I'm going to the beach, I put my camera in a seal-up freezer bag and place it in my camera bag with a freezer pack to keep it all cool. I ensure my hands are absolutely sand-free before I remove the camera.

Sand in your camera leads to very expensive repairs. And if you drop your camera in saltwater you may as well throw it away – it is irreparable. If you cannot be sure of making your camera beach-safe you should use disposable cameras.

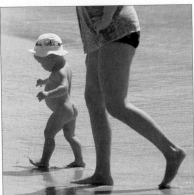

■ **This is a typical beach snapshot,** *but a safe one. I shot it on my underwater point-and-shoot. That way there was no risk of sand or saltwater damage.*

Travel themes and obsessions

MANY TRAVEL PHOTOGRAPHERS get locked into recurrent themes that can become quite obsessive. I have to confess to having a bit of a thing about markets and roads – I have taken loads of shots of both. I have a photographer friend who is hooked on doors. He has shot thousands of doors all over the world.

But seriously, to find a subject that really interests you on your travels can lead to a unique set of pictures that will prove very satisfying.

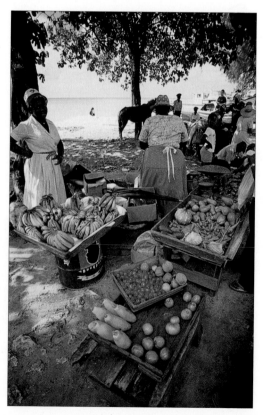

■ **I'm hooked** on markets. I used a 24mm lens for this one in Barbados, so that I could look down onto the produce. It also provided me with an attractive perspective composition.

When you get home

We have always collected lots of little bits and pieces on our travels that have become family memorabilia. I often use the objects to make still-life studies when I get home – sometimes months later. It's great fun and brings back loads of memories.

■ **Michelle came home** *from Italy with a big collection of pasta – every colour imaginable for pasta dishes of every type. She composed them on a light-box, which has captured the translucent quality of the subject.*

A simple summary

✓ Before booking your holiday do plenty of research. Plan what you are going to shoot and when.

✓ Make sure your camera works. If it doesn't, buy a new one.

✓ Don't let photography cause grief for the family – it's their break too!

✓ Women should research the female role in countries they visit and act appropriately. It seems medieval but can save any hassle.

✓ Take appropriate clothing for the climate as well as for the type of days you have planned, whether walking, driving, or whatever.

✓ If you want to photograph the locals, ask them first and be ready. Reward their kindness by ensuring they don't have to wait.

✓ If underwater photography is your thing, be aware of safety concerns and never go out diving alone.

PART FIVE

ARE YOU READY FOR THE DIGITAL WORLD?

TAKING THINGS MORE SERIOUSLY

THIS LAST SECTION OF THE BOOK is really about whetting your appetite for more and inspiring you to go on further than you perhaps first thought you would. Some of this section is an *insight* into how professional photographers work and the equipment they use, but there's also information about black-and-white photography, details on what happens *behind the scenes* after your roll of film is finished, as well as a fact or two to shed some light on digital photography.

I won't go into detail on darkroom techniques or the use of camera movements on a 5 x 4 monorail camera. But you can *advance your knowledge* from this book's starting point by further reading or night classes. Just get out there and do it!

Chapter 21

Medium and Large Formats

DO WE REALLY NEED THE EXTRA HASSLE of large, heavy cameras? What are these strange, antiquated machines used for? And why? Medium and large format cameras are still very much in use by professionals, and they have a serious fan base among amateurs too. This chapter looks at these cameras in depth and reveals the benefits, and otherwise, of going it large.

In this chapter...

✓ Why go larger than 35mm?

✓ Medium format cameras

✓ Large format cameras

✓ Comparative image sizes

Why go larger than 35mm?

THE MOST OBVIOUS DIFFERENCE *between a 35mm camera and medium and large format cameras is that the medium and large formats produce bigger negatives (or transparencies).*

The larger negative size then produces a sharper, finer-grained print because it requires less enlargement to produce a bigger image. Professional photographers, who don't require the speed of handling that 35mm cameras provide, go for medium format cameras for the extra quality and control that they can achieve.

Medium format cameras

THE TERM MEDIUM FORMAT *photography describes photography undertaken on any camera in between 35mm and 5 x 4-inch large format. The medium format camera is the workhorse of the professional. The original classic medium format is the 6 x 6 cm, or 2¼ x 2¼ inch.*

Initially, the Rolleiflex twin lens reflex (TLR) camera was the standard – in fact, they are still on the market – but the Rolls-Royce of medium formats is the SLR Hasselblad – very expensive, but superbly built and designed.

The other medium format cameras available include the following:

- 6 x 7 cm, made by Mamiya and Pentax
- 6 x 4.5 cm, by Pentax, Mamiya, and Bronica
- 6 x 8 cm, by Fuji
- 6 x 9 cm, by Linhof

MAMIYA SLR

Common to all medium format cameras is the 120mm film. Unlike 35mm or APS films, the 120mm is a roll of film wound around a spool that is underwoven with paper.

Quick roll change

One big attraction of medium format cameras is that they are mostly of modular construction, that is, the camera itself is a separate box. The film is therefore loaded into a magazine that clips on to the back of the camera. This means that you can have several magazines with both colour and black-and-white loaded and change your choice of film quickly mid-roll. You can also buy Polaroid® magazines for most medium format cameras. Professionals use Polaroids as a test before making their final exposure.

I use a Hasselblad for black-and-whites when I want a smooth, fine-grained image – for example, on portraits and landscapes.

But although the medium formats can produce such high quality, that doesn't mean that they are better than 35mm cameras. The 35mm is faster to use, more convenient, and lighter. I would never think of using a Hasselblad for reportage or sport, for instance.

Focusing hood

HASSELBLAD MEDIUM FORMAT CAMERA

Film magazine

Focusing ring

Aperture ring

Shutter ring

Frame counter | Film-advance winder | Shutter button

A great-value way of getting into medium format photography is through the recent rangefinder 6 x 4.5-cm cameras. You look through a viewfinder just like with a point-and-shoot.

INTERNET

www.phototechmag.com/previous-articles/sept99-mort.htm

This great article, on PHOTO Techniques *magazine's web site, sings the praises of 6 x 6-cm photography.*

Large format cameras

THE SIGHT OF A PHOTOGRAPHER *half-hidden by a big black cloth and gazing through a bulky, ancient-looking camera sounds like an historical flashback (or an hysterical flashback), but that's not the case. Large format cameras shooting 5 x 4- or 10 x 8-inch film are still used today. Many of the top advertising photographers use large format (often with colour transparency film) as their main tool of the trade.*

Many of the greatest landscape pictures that are fixed into our memories were shot on 10 x 8 cameras. Large format cameras are heavy and almost always need to be supported on a tripod, but the photographers lugged these great loads up mountains and down the other side. The rewards were prints of magnificent quality due to the huge negatives they shot. Many landscape specialists still use large format, but usually the less bulky 5 x 4.

I started off shooting press-type photography on a 5 x 4 press camera. Because shooting was rather slow, I had to plan my pictures carefully, which I think was good training.

Whereas a 50mm lens is considered normal on a 35mm camera, 150mm is a normal lens for a 5 x 4. And because of the longer lenses that are required by 5 x 4 cameras, they also require more light to achieve a depth of focus comparable to that of a 35mm camera.

Take your time

Shooting large format requires a much different philosophy to shooting on either medium or 35mm formats. A slower, more contemplative attitude is needed. These cameras are slow to operate but, with the large, ground-glass viewing screen, you can compose your shots very carefully and see the image very big and clear.

But large format photography has another control advantage appreciated by many pros. Each exposure is on a separate sheet of film; this means that each can be given individual processing attention, which is very difficult on a roll of 120mm or 35mm film.

Trivia...

When I was a young photographer in Melbourne, Australia, the quality of the printing in magazines was so poor that clients often demanded 10 x 8-inch transparencies to reproduce from. I can tell you from my own experience that trying to photograph hyperactive kids on 10 x 8 was an absolute nightmare!

The themes that best suit large format photography are still life, architecture and industrial shots, and landscapes.

Large format types

There are basically three types of large format camera: the monorail (or view camera), the flatbed (or field camera), and the press camera.

Monorail (view camera)

This is the most simple of all camera constructions. At the base of the camera is, as its name suggests, a single rail. At the front and back are two either L-shaped or, more usually, U-shaped brackets that support the lens (at the front) as well as the ground-glass viewing screen and film holder. Between the lens and the viewing screen is a light-tight bellows. The brackets can slide up and down and across the rail in order to focus the camera, and they can also be swung in a circular motion. These up, down, and swivel actions are called camera movements. The camera movements are used to control perspective and depth of focus.

Lens   Lens panel   Bellows   Film holder

Ground-glass viewing screen

L-shaped bracket

Monorail

Cable release

■ **The monorail** *is the ultimate professional-studio, large format camera offering the maximum number of lens movements.*

Flatbed (field cameras)

Flatbed cameras do the same job as monorails but are more compact and lighter, making them a better choice for location work. The disadvantage is that they don't offer the same amount of movement control as the monorail.

Rear swing and rising back controls

Carrying strap

Bellows

Aperture control

Lens panel

Shutter mechanism

Lens

Front swing and rising front controls

Lateral lens movement controls

Rear focusing knob

Front focusing knob

Flatbed base

WITHOUT RISING FRONT

WITH RISING FRONT

■ **The flatbed camera** *has most of the same functions as the monorail but has fewer movement and lens-extension possibilities. It is also lighter and more portable, making it a popular choice for location work, especially for architecture and garden photography.*

Gandolfi (UK) and Deardorf (US) still make beautiful field cameras from wood and brass. You can choose your own woodgrain and fittings, and many pros have them made to order.

Press camera

This is the sort of camera you'll see in the old black-and-white movies, with a flash and photographer attached. It was the original press photographer's camera. Some have a rising front and limited movements built in. If you are interested in 5 x 4 large format photography, look out for one of these in second-hand shops: they are a very inexpensive way of entering the large format world. And with the great choice of lenses available you can produce images of incredible quality for a very small investment.

Back movement control

Accessory bracket

Bellows

Back movement control

Rising front control

Handgrip (often includes shutter release)

Rangefinder

Rising front control

Back movement control

Lens

Lens panel

Back movement control

Focusing knob

Extension rail

Bellows adjustment control

■ The press camera *offers a rather limited number of lens movements, but it is quick to operate and very durable.*

Nearly all large format cameras have the lenses mounted on detachable lens boards that clip on and off the front of the camera.

I really feel that whether you use large format or not depends a great deal on your temperament. If you favour the more contemplative approach of a painter, then 5 x 4 or 10 x 8 cameras may be for you. If, on the other hand, you want to capture life's hustle and bustle, forget large format. Life will have hustled and bustled past you before you even have the camera properly attached to the tripod.

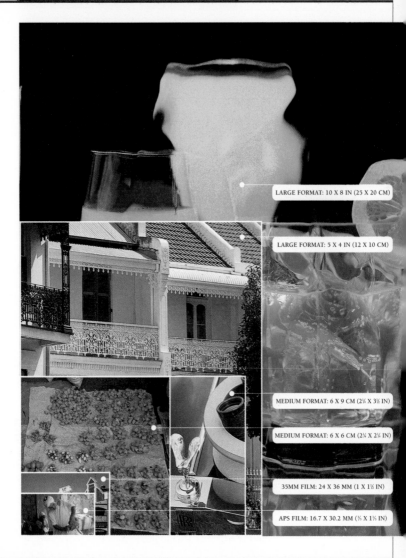

LARGE FORMAT: 10 X 8 IN (25 X 20 CM)

LARGE FORMAT: 5 X 4 IN (12 X 10 CM)

MEDIUM FORMAT: 6 X 9 CM (2¼ X 3½ IN)

MEDIUM FORMAT: 6 X 6 CM (2¼ X 2¼ IN)

35MM FILM: 24 X 36 MM (1 X 1½ IN)

APS FILM: 16.7 X 30.2 MM (⅔ X 1⅕ IN)

Comparative image sizes

TO EXPLAIN the differences between the formats available, I thought it might be useful to show you the actual size of the negative or transparency that each one produces. More importantly, you can see the relative sizes.

Check out the size difference between an APS negative and that of a 10 x 8. The quality difference is relative to the size difference, so size does matter! It makes sense: you can't expect a tiny APS neg to produce a 35 x 28-cm (14 x 11-inch) print as sharp and fine-grained as a 10 x 8 neg will.

A simple summary

✓ The increased size of negatives and transparencies produced by medium and large format cameras means better quality images.

✓ The medium format camera is the choice of professionals.

✓ Medium format cameras come in various sizes from several different manufacturers, but all use 120mm film.

✓ Large format cameras are heavy and almost always need a tripod.

✓ Large format cameras use longer lenses than 35mm cameras and so need more light to achieve a comparable depth of focus.

Chapter 22

Seeing in Black-and-White

I CAN'T ATTEMPT IN THIS CHAPTER to teach you about black-and-white photography in any great depth: that requires another book devoted to the subject. This chapter is a taster – I'm going to point you in the direction of the possibilities and hopefully inspire you to take the subject further. Fifty per cent of the quality of a black-and-white image is achieved in the darkroom, so if you are going to get into black-and-white, you should also try to get into developing and printing your own black-and-white film. (Or you can, of course, make black-and-white prints on your computer.) To start with, though, you can get your minilab to print your black-and-white efforts and see how you like them.

In this chapter...
- ✓ *Two-tone visualization*
- ✓ *Black-and-white technique*
- ✓ *The darkroom*

BLACK-AND-WHITE PHOTOGRAPHY CAN MAKE SOME SUBJECTS LOOK EERIE

Two-tone visualization

WE LIVE IN A COLOURFUL WORLD. *Our reality is colour, so the moment we load a black-and-white film into our camera we are taking a step away from reality. We don't naturally see the world in monochromatic tones, so black-and-white photography is, in a sense, an abstraction.*

Oddly enough, black-and-white news and photojournalism pictures have always had the reputation of being the real thing, the most powerful interpretation of events.

Many of the definitive photographs from our recent history have been black-and-white, so I suppose black-and-white is buried in our mind as the medium of news and current affairs. Black-and-white has also made a great comeback in fashionable art photography, and you see more black-and-white images in the trendy magazines than you did a few years ago.

To work well in black-and-white you have to develop a new way of seeing. You need to learn to visualize your world of colour in shades of grey. To get some idea of how colours convert to black-and-white, try fiddling with the controls on your TV, changing the picture constantly from colour to black-and-white. After a while you will recognize what density of grey various colours convert to.

DEFINITION

*The term **tonal management** describes a photographer's ability to compose a picture to achieve a pleasing arrangement of tones.*

Where the success or failure of a colour picture is dependent on colour management, in black-and-white work it depends on **tonal management**.

■ **I first envisaged** *this Stockholm scene as a colour picture (right), and it wasn't until later, when I walked past the same spot again, that I decided to take a black-and-white picture of it, too (opposite).*

■ **I think this has made** *a stronger image in black-and-white than in colour. The light had moved slightly and the window was now more obviously highlighted. My composition is stronger in this picture also. The window makes a fine focal point, and the monochromatic tones lend themselves well to black-and-white.*

Black-and-white technique

THE TECHNIQUE OF BLACK-AND-WHITE *photography is based on a knowledge of how to manipulate the tonal contrast of the subject that you frame in the viewfinder. There are several variables that influence contrast, and we will look at them here.*

Light

The quality of light and the angle at which it falls on the subject are the first, and most important, elements in changing or controlling the tonal contrasts in a picture. (For more information on this, see chapters 10 and 11.)

Choice of film

The slower the film, the higher its inherent contrast, and the faster the film, the lower its inherent contrast. So if you want to take a very "contrasty" shot of, say, a beach scene, you would choose a 50–100 ISO film. Or if you need a soft, moody picture of a foggy morning, you would go for a fast 1000–3200 ISO film.

■ **The cross-light** *has brought out all the character lines in this artist's face, helping me to capture the intensity of the man. The shadow adds some mystery.*

Development

Some developers give a more contrasty finish than others. A general rule is that if you want to increase the contrast, you underexpose the film and compensate by increasing the development time. So you could rate a 400 ISO film at 1200 ISO and increase the development time according to the manufacturer's instructions. You will then have pushed the film 1½ stops and, in so doing, created a *hard neg*. Conversely, if you exposed a 400 ISO film at 200 ISO and decreased the development time accordingly, you will have pulled the film 1 stop and so softened the contrast of the neg.

DEFINITION

*A **hard neg** is the term given to a high-contrast negative. A low-contrast neg is called a soft neg.*

Remember to mark the film immediately whenever you push or pull it. You might forget later and develop it incorrectly or give the lab the wrong instructions.

Filtration

This can have a dramatic effect on contrast. In black-and-white photography, a filter lightens the tonal reproduction of colours at its own end of the spectrum and darkens the tones of colours at the opposite end. Take, for example, a red-brick house in a green field where the sky above is a perfect blue. A red filter will lighten the house and darken the sky and field when shot on black-and-white film. The increase in contrast will be immense. The effect will be less marked if we were to use an orange filter. With the red filter the house will be almost white and the sky almost black, whereas the orange filter will convert the tones to light grey and dark grey. If we use a blue or green filter, the opposite effect would be apparent: an almost white sky, a pale grey field, and a dark grey house. The densities of grey will depend on how strong the green and blue filters are.

■ **These two pictures** *demonstrate the dramatic effect that filtration can have on black-and-white photography. This top picture was shot using a light orange filter. There is some separation in the tones.*

■ **After taking** *the picture above, I quickly changed to a deep red filter. The contrast has increased considerably, resulting in the more dramatic print seen here.*

Paper

In the darkroom we have another chance to alter the contrast of the picture. The contrast of multigrade or variable-contrast papers can be altered by using a series of filters over the lens that go from 0, which is very soft, to 6, which is very hard.

■ **I have chosen these three pictures** to show how you can alter the contrast of your pictures at the printing stage by changing the contrast of your multigrade filter. Left to right: grade 1, grade 3, grade 5.

You can buy multigrade heads for your enlarger. These allow you to adjust the contrast filtration.

Aperture

Your choice of aperture can have a great effect on the tonal make-up of the picture. If you stop down and keep the image sharp for both foreground and background, the tonal effect will be to keep the tones sharp and more separated than if you open the aperture to wide open. The narrow depth of focus means that the out-of-focus foreground and/or background will produce the effect of the tonal separation to be softened. Therefore, the tones will tend to merge together.

INTERNET

www.photogs.com/bwworld

The Black-and-White World web site describes itself as "a celebration of photography". There are informative articles, some great black-and-white pictures, and tips to help you improve your own work.

Shutter speed

Your choice of shutter speed will have a similar effect on tonal separation as aperture. If you use a fast shutter speed, the tones of the moving subject will be crisp and sharply defined. But on a slow shutter speed the subject will be blurred, and so will the tones: they will merge together.

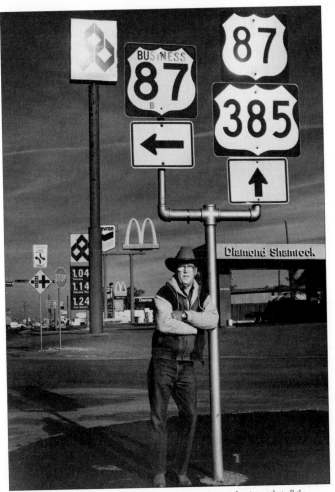

■ **I have used depth of focus here** *because it was important to the picture that all the background signs were sharp. I took this photograph on a Hasselblad 6 x 6 with a 50mm lens; I added a red filter to increase the contrast and, therefore, the drama.*

The darkroom

I HAVE BEEN DEVELOPING and printing my own black-and-white photography for about 40 years (I never thought I'd be saying that!), and I am even more enthusiastic about printing now than I was when I first started. It follows, then, that I am very keen to encourage you to try it for yourself. If you are a computer enthusiast, you will probably opt for learning to print on your PC or Mac, but I don't believe you can match the superb quality of a fine, traditional bromide print. And anyway, the peace you get locked away in the darkroom, undisturbed, is just heaven!

Recent technology has dramatically simplified the making of prints. Traditional printing paper was made by coating a silver bromide photographic emulsion onto paper. The print then required 45 minutes of washing in running water and needed to be placed in a print dryer to ensure it ended up flat. Now we have *RC paper*, which has a plastic base. RC paper requires just 2 minutes of washing and you can dry it by just hanging it on a line. This means that, although still very convenient, running water is no longer absolutely essential in printing. You can wash by just changing the water several times.

> **DEFINITION**
>
> *The RC in **RC paper** stands for resin-coated. Most printmakers still use a paper-based material called fibre-based, or FB, paper.*

One size fits all!

The traditional papers were graded, so you had to buy a whole packet or box of paper for each degree of contrast running from grade 1 (soft) up to grade 5 (hard). This made printing an expensive pursuit. Now, though, with multigrade, or variable contrast, papers, you only need to buy one box and you can change the contrast by using filters.

Getting it together

To get started with a darkroom is really not very expensive. But you do need a room that is light-tight and, even more importantly, dustproof. Dust is Public Enemy No. 1.

Never clean your darkroom with a broom or a duster. You will lift the dust into the air. Just wipe slowly with a damp cloth.

You could convert your bathroom into a temporary darkroom, but that can cause problems with the rest of the family. An unused cupboard or shed is better. You'll use your darkroom more often if you have a permanent set-up.

WHAT YOU NEED

Printing your own black-and-whites isn't expensive, but these are the essential items:

- A safe light
- A film-development tank and spirals
- Darkroom trays (at least three) to process and wash prints
- A thermometer
- An enlarger
- A masking board
- A measuring jug

Your major investment out of all of these is the enlarger, which can cost anything from £100 to £2,000 – but they never go out of date. I still use an enlarger that I bought 30 years ago. The only addition I've made is the multigrade head, which is not essential. Most of the cost of the enlarger goes on the quality of the lens. I recommend you buy a well-built enlarger with a good lens. Once you've got your enlarger you can get all the rest for about £150 or so. I don't have the space in this book to teach you darkroom technique, but there are lots of part-time courses you can take to learn the basics, and I urge you to do just that. Good luck!

A simple summary

✓ We see the world in colour so, for black-and-white photography, we must learn how colours translate into shades of grey.

✓ Black-and-white technique is based on manipulating tones.

✓ Tonal contrast is influenced by light, film, development of the film, filtration, printing paper, aperture, and shutter.

✓ To appreciate black-and-white photography to its full you should print your own pictures.

✓ The cost of printing is far lower than it used to be, so there's really no excuse not to try it!

Chapter 23

Working with Your Photofinisher

THE PHOTOFINISHER is the descriptive title given to the outfit that develops and prints your films. Other names used are laboratory (or lab), process house, minilab, and D&P (developing and printing) house. The photofinishing business has become very competitive in recent years and that has meant an improvement in service and print quality. Before we get into detail, I want to stress that, no matter how in control you are of your camera, it's the photofinisher's work that you're presented with at the end of the day. So take the time to find the best photofinisher in your area and build up a good relationship with the staff.

In this chapter...
- ✓ It's a photofinish!
- ✓ Choosing a lab
- ✓ The minilab
- ✓ The custom lab
- ✓ An alternative?

WORK HAND-IN-HAND WITH YOUR MINILAB TO GET THE BEST RESULTS

It's a photofinish!

SO... YOU'VE FINISHED YOUR ROLL OF FILM, *rewound it (or the camera's automatically done it for you), and removed it. The next step, unless you're developing your own black-and-whites, is to take it to the minilab for developing and processing. But what goes on there?*

What you take to be developed is film with a *latent image* on it. The lab develops the film from the visible negative, or neg.

> **DEFINITION**
>
> *The **latent image** is the invisible image made by the chemical reaction of light on the film's emulsion.*

It's important to understand that a negative can be printed in a multitude of ways: light or dark; with or without colour casts; it can have different contrasts; and it can be printed on different surfaces – glossy, matt, semi-matt – and at various sizes. This all makes a difference. The negative is only a starting point, and it can be interpreted however you like.

Never get fingerprints on your negatives; when handling negs hold them by the edges.

NEGATIVES SHOULD BE PROTECTED

Choosing a lab

THESE DAYS YOU HAVE AN ENORMOUS CHOICE *of places where you can take your film to be developed. You can go to your local chemist's or newsagent's, you can pop the film in the post and get your prints sent back a few days later, or you can take it to one of the specialist, and therefore more expensive, developing shops in your local town centre.*

The mass-production labs – the ones that your supermarket and chemist send your films to – have their machines set to automatically produce an average, standard, "okay" print. The best of these labs do a good job and, because they handle thousands of rolls of film every day, they are cheaper than the specialist shops, or minilabs.

The minilab

I PREFER TO ENTRUST MY FILMS to one of my local minilabs. A minilab is one that has its own machine in the shop. They can be found even in small towns of late. The advantage of the minilab is that you can discuss your processing and prints with the technician who will be operating the machine. The minilab technician can override the machine's automatic settings to produce a more individual print to your own specifications.

I did a test with three rolls of 12-exposure film. On each film, I shot the same subjects in the same conditions, and I sent each roll to a different lab. One lab was definitely the best, so I stuck with it.

Communicating with your lab's staff

Getting the best results from your minilab often comes down to your relationship with the technician. Try to find a lab that you can communicate with and where the staff really care about producing good prints.

If the lab staff are arrogant and don't want to spend time discussing your work, find a different lab.

Minilabs are more expensive but worth it if you can find a good one. A good minilab will have a large selection of film, and the staff should be able to advise you not only on which film to choose but on other photographic topics too.

If the lab claims it's impossible to make a good print from your neg, ask the technician to point out the problem on the neg. If he's right, you'll get a useful lesson... and if he's bluffing, change labs.

If you have been shooting colour in fluorescent or tungsten light, tell the lab and they can adjust the machine to compensate for the colour cast. With the best will in the world, minilabs cannot change the balance of contrast in a print. If the sky has printed too light but the countryside is perfect, the minilab cannot change that. In order to get that degree of individual attention, you'll need to use a custom lab, or pro lab.

Printing, whether in colour or black-and-white, is a great skill. There are some printers who are as famous in their field as photographers.

TAKING CONTROL

Your lab, or photofinisher, can do a lot more for you than just a straight print. But you need to be in control and tell the staff what you want. Apart from having an unsatisfactory print redone, what little tweaks here or there would make your shot more pleasing? If you don't have a relationship with your minilab in which you can discuss your prints, find one that's more interested in its customers.

Changing colour tones

Your minilab can dramatically change the colour tones of your print, but only at one end of the spectrum per print. The machine can be programmed to make a print bluer or redder, for example, but it can't do both on the same print.

■ **This is the pier** *on Sanibel Island, Florida. The print above is what I originally received back from the lab. I asked the technician to add a bit more red, since I felt that the scene was more red when I shot it (although it probably wasn't, in fact). The result is the print opposite, which I like much more.*

Black-and-white tones

Now that it's had such a revival, most labs also do a
black-and-white service, but we don't have to end up
with straight black-and-white prints. The machine
can be programmed to produce beautifully toned
prints that are comparable in colour to darkroom-
produced, traditional toning – without the effort!
Don't go mad though, keep the tones subtle: in
other words, retain the black-and-white quality.

■ **These four prints** *were all
made by an automatic minilab
machine from a black-and-white
neg. Explain to the technician that
you want tones, not solid colours.*

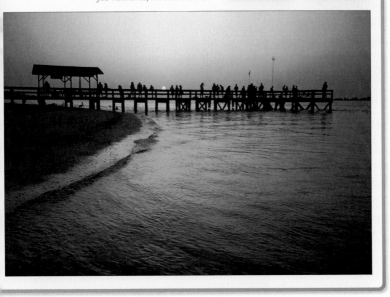

The custom lab

CUSTOM, OR PRO, LABS ARE ONLY FOUND in towns and cities large enough to have a community of professional photographers. Here you can get your prints made individually by hand. The printer at a custom lab can change the contrast by adding more exposure to small areas of the print or by shading small areas of the print to make it lighter – for example, if you have a face that's in the shade.

Of course, all this extra time and attention costs money. The custom lab is more expensive but for that special picture or for a beautiful blow-up of your favourite person, pet, or scene, why not try the choice of professionals?

Before you order a big blow-up, make sure the neg is really sharp – the printer or minilab technician will help you check. In a big print, lack of focus will show up... big time.

■ **The swan picture** *above is the original print I received from the minilab. The machine made an average exposure, but the tonal range was too great for it to cope, so I had it reprinted at a custom lab. They were able to add more exposure to the swans in the foreground. The result was the print on the right.*

An alternative?

THERE IS ANOTHER ALTERNATIVE to the minilab and the pro lab, and that's the photo kiosk. You might find one of these in a supermarket or even inside your local minilab.

Here you can crop your images as you fancy and play with colour and tone to your heart's content. The resulting prints have a different feel and quality to photographic prints, but they can be quite interesting and are definitely worth a try.

INTERNET

www.snappysnaps.com

This is the web site of Snappy Snaps, the high-street minilab, which in 2000 became the first company to receive Amateur Photographer's "High Street Lab of the Year" award in five successive years.

A simple summary

✓ The negative that your camera produces can be printed in many ways by varying the contrast, colour cast, size, and even printing surface.

✓ These days there are many places in your local high street that will develop and print your pictures for you.

✓ Minilabs are developing and printing shops that have their own machine and experienced technicians in-store.

✓ Often you will get the best results from your minilab by communicating your needs to the technicians.

✓ Don't stick with a minilab if you aren't happy with its service – there are plenty more that would be glad of your custom.

✓ Custom, or pro, labs, only found in large towns, are the most expensive option, but they are worth considering if you want a very special print made.

Chapter 24

Digital Photography

DO YOU KNOW YOUR PIXELS from your RAMs? Your CD-ROMs from your hard drives? Well, if you do – if you are a 21st-century, computer-literate person to whom the mobile phone and the PC are vital, life-sustaining pieces of equipment – then you already have a great start when it comes to digital photography. I must confess that I'm a student myself in this technology and have had to do some study and practice in order to pass on some sound advice to you guys.

In this chapter...
✓ What exactly is digital photography?
✓ The cameras
✓ Let's talk about pixels
✓ What do I do with my images?
✓ How does the quality compare?

What exactly is digital photography?

AT ITS MOST BASIC LEVEL, digital photography is the same as conventional photography – that is, they both make an image by drawing light through a lens into a light-tight box.

■ **The basic function** of a digital camera is the same as that of a 19th-century daguerreotype camera – to record the world around you as a photograph.

The big difference is that, instead of capturing the image on film, a digital camera uses electronic sensors. The sensors convert the light into various electronic charges that are converted into computer language or code and recorded on to a microchip.

Digital cameras are more fragile than analogue ones. Extreme heat, humidity, or even just a bump can cause serious damage.

Mass production

Loaded with the electronic code of a digital photograph, you can produce an image that (with the help of the right software) you can manipulate to your heart's content, without getting your hands wet or turning off the lights. You can also reproduce the image identically as many times as you wish from the digital file.

I'm sure that even though some people – and it's mostly a generation thing – have a bit of a technology blockage and therefore don't want to get involved in digital, there are millions of others whose interest in photography could well have been sparked by their computer – and that's good news. The other piece of very good news is that, generally speaking, shooting digital is much the same as shooting on film. If you can shoot beautiful pictures on a conventional camera, you can also do it on a digital camera; the working techniques feel pretty much the same.

All the major news agencies use digital cameras now. It means that a news picture taken in New Zealand can be up on a newspaper editor's computer monitor in London just seconds later.

The cameras

AS WITH TRADITIONAL CAMERAS, in the digital world you get what you pay for. The decision you make on price, therefore, determines the quality of image you will produce. And what you want to produce will mainly be dependent on what you intend to do with the images once you have recorded them.

> **DEFINITION**
>
> The easiest way to define a **pixel** is to think of it as one tile of a Roman wall mosaic, in which each tile has only one colour, but when all the tiles are creatively arranged, you have a complete picture.

If you only want to view your pictures on your computer screen, e-mail them to friends or business associates, or use them on your web site, then you don't need a high-resolution camera. A camera with 640 x 480 *pixels* would suffice.

Even at the cheaper end of the digital market you get an LCD screen to play back your images. You also have a viewfinder, like that on a point-and-shoot camera, a fixed memory (or storage capacity), and a fixed-focal-length lens.

I would advise you to go for a digital camera with a removable memory card; this may cost a little more but it adds flexibility.

If your budget is a little bigger and you think you will want to move on to producing some reasonable-quality prints later, then you need to buy more pixels, a zoom lens of better quality, and an LCD screen to guide your playback facility. Make sure you get a good, clear LCD, because the quality does vary between the various makes and models.

Increasing quality

If you're really going to go for it and you want high-quality A4- or even A3-size prints, you need to go top-of-the-range – and you're looking at more than just more pixels. In money terms, that will mean a price comparable to a top-of-the-range conventional SLR. One of the best cameras currently available in this price range will enable you to shoot 21 consecutive shots at 4½ frames per second and has shutter speeds from 30 seconds to ¹⁄₁₆₀₀ of a second. It has fast autofocus, and the flash synchronizes at ¹⁄₅₀₀ of a second.

■ **The LCD screen** on a digital camera is enormously useful, but you should use the normal viewfinder as much as possible to save draining your batteries unnecessarily.

315

What do digital cameras do better?

There are several great things about digital cameras, and these include their compatibility with the computer, which enables you to e-mail pictures around the world in seconds, print up a load of instant postcards (if you have a printer, of course), or show them on your TV or computer monitor. Also, you can record up to 500 images on your memory card (I'll discuss this further later), which is like having a 500-exposure film in your camera. And, of course, you can manipulate your pictures to produce an infinite number of visually differing versions of your original.

Remember that although initial expenditure on a digital camera is more than in conventional photography, you have no more film costs or lab costs to pay for.

■ **One of the great things** *about digital images is that you don't have to look at them as prints. You can view them on your TV or computer monitor, for example.*

What are digital cameras not so good at?

The main problem with digital cameras is the delay between pushing the button and the camera writing the image to memory. For my kind of photography, which is mostly photojournalistic and relies on catching a "magic moment", digital is just not fast enough yet. Plus the start-up time delay between switching the camera on and being ready to record images is also a big problem.

Some of the more recent top-of-the-range cameras have shortened both the image-capture delay and the start-up time, closing the gap between digital and analogue, but these delays are still a factor.

The print quality is still not as good from a high-priced digital camera as it is from a low-priced point-and-shoot. And producing a black-and-white exhibition-quality print that approaches the quality of a fine bromide print requires a huge investment in equipment. One final point is that you don't have the control over depth of focus that you do with conventional cameras.

Let's talk about pixels

WHEREAS TRADITIONAL PHOTOGRAPHIC IMAGES *are recorded*
on light-sensitive photographic film, digital images are recorded on a sensor
made up of pixels. The quality of image that a digital camera is capable of
depends on the number of pixels it incorporates.

Whereas most 35mm cameras record on 24 x 36-mm (1 x 1½-inch)
film, a digital camera records on a sensor measured in pixels. An
example might be a rectangular 2,048 x 1,536 pixels, giving a total
of 3.34 million pixels, or 3.34 *megapixels*, or *MPs*.

> **DEFINITION**
>
> A **megapixel**, *or* **MP**, *is one*
> *million pixels.*

More pixels = better quality

If you just intend to use your images for publishing on the Internet or viewing on your
monitor, you can make do with a camera with a 640 x 480 pixel resolution, which will
cost about the same as a mid-priced compact camera. But if you want to produce good-
quality prints, you really need 1,600 x 1,200 pixels of resolution (around 2 MPs). The
top-of-the-range digital cameras are currently boasting 4 MPs and rising all the time.
So, to get high-quality prints, look for a camera with loads of pixels.

However, pixels are not the only
consideration when it comes to image
quality. The quality of the lens is vitally
important, and, at the other end,
the quality of the printer is just as
important. So if you are looking to
produce digitally created prints
that compare with traditionally
created prints, you need to
make a serious
investment.

■ **One of the most**
important considerations
when buying a digital camera
is the quality of the lens. Go
for the best you can afford.

What do I do with my images?

THE LOWEST-PRICED DIGITAL CAMERAS have a fixed memory
built into the camera. The problem with that is that when you have filled the
memory with pictures you have to download the images.

You can take up to 60 photographs
on a fixed-memory camera before
downloading for storage on your
computer hard drive, Zip®
disk, or CD. You should
also make back-up
copies of all your work.

The limitations of a fixed storage
capacity are obvious. You need your
computer handy at all times and that means
there's a big time gap before you can start
shooting again.

ZIP DRIVE

The mid-priced and expensive models have memory cards that store images and can
be replaced when full, just like a film. So if you are on holiday or want to take lots of
shots, you just buy a few memory cards and keep shooting.

Storage capacity on memory cards can vary dramatically. Some hold
more than 300 images. Make sure you know which card is compatible
with your camera and what its capacity is.

Alternatively, if you are happy enough to put your faith in e-mail, you could send the images to your computer at home, where they'll be waiting for your return, wipe your memory card clean, and start shooting again.

You can even bypass the computer altogether and plug your camera directly into the printer.

Another way to save digital images is to plug your camera into your VCR and record the pictures on to videotape.

DIGITAL MEMORY SYSTEMS

There are two systems used to record, and temporarily store, your pictures in camera. The cheapest is a built-in memory that can't be expanded. A more flexible alternative is a removable memory card: once a card is full you can either download it straight away and reuse the card, or you can replace it with another card and download later.

The names of the removable memory cards vary between manufacturers and include Compact Flash and Memory Stick. When buying extra cards make sure you get the correct type for your camera.

■ **Compact Flash** *is the memory card used by the largest number of manufacturers.*

■ **Memory Stick** *is the name Sony gives to its own digital camera memory cards.*

How does the quality compare?

ONE OF THE BIGGEST PROBLEMS with digital cameras has been that their sensitivity to light has only been about the equivalent of that of a 100 ISO film. This has meant that you could only produce good-quality images in bright light without using flash.

Some of the latest top-of-the-range cameras, however, offer the equivalent of 200, 400, 800, and even 1600 ISO. On the down side, there's a fall-off in quality and increase in *noise* as the light sensitivity increases, but it's an improvement on previous cameras.

As we move forward in time, other big technological advances are the reduced start-up and shutter-delay times. Digital cameras are closing the gap on traditional cameras in regards to their ease of use and quality of image.

> **DEFINITION**
>
> **Noise** is digital jargon meaning a break-up of the image, similar to grain on film or interference on your TV screen.

Scanning prints

Despite all this, at the time of writing, my personal feelings are that if you are already the proud owner of a good-quality 35mm camera, why not originate your pictures on film and scan the negs or prints? I'll tell you more about this in the next chapter.

■ **I shot this picture** with a digital camera. I set the aperture to f6.3 and the shutter speed to ¹/₃₂₀ of a second. I was only 20 cm (8 inches) from the poppy, so I used the macro mode to ensure it was in focus.

INTERNET

www.dpreview.com

This is a great web site for those of you thinking about buying a digital camera. Unbiased, in-depth reviews of most of the current models can be found here.

■ **For this photograph** *I set the digital camera's aperture to f2 and selected a shutter speed of ½₀₀ of a second. I used the exposure compensation to ensure the subject wasn't underexposed due to the bright light coming through the window.*

A simple summary

✓ The purposes of digital and conventional photography are the same – to record the world around us. And, essentially, the way they work is the same too.

✓ Conventional photography records images on to film; digital records to a microchip.

✓ With the right software, digital photographs can be manipulated on a computer and exact copies of your final image can be made time and time again.

✓ As always – in terms of number of pixels, LCD screens, and lenses – you get what you pay for.

✓ Cameras that use removable memory cards are more costly than those with a fixed memory but are far more convenient.

✓ You should always back up your images on to a storage medium.

✓ The quality of digital is not as good as conventional, but it's getting there.

Chapter 25

The Digital Darkroom

THESE DAYS WE USE COMPUTERS to do a great many things for us, or rather the computer is the tool that seems to be increasingly indispensable for performing our daily tasks. So it's only natural that we extend this list of tasks to our photography... I guess! In this last chapter we'll look at the computer's role in 21st-century photography and what equipment you need in order to buy into this revolution. I'll also show you some digital work created by a couple of friends of mine.

In this chapter...

- ✓ Photography and your computer
- ✓ Which computer to choose?
- ✓ Peripherals
- ✓ Case study: Graeme Harris
- ✓ Case study: Maud Larsson

PHOTOGRAPHY DOESN'T HAVE TO REFLECT ACCURATELY WHAT YOU SEE

Photography and your computer

SOME PEOPLE FEEL THREATENED by the computer as a producer of photographic images, and some see it as a sacred gift that will set us free. I see it as a fantastic new tool that can offer more creative possibilities to photographers.

The computer can certainly set you free from chemicals and darkrooms. It allows you to manipulate and print in minutes an image that could take hours in the darkroom. Also, once your file is stored, you can reproduce your print at the press of a button to make an identical copy.

For me, the point of a digital print is that it isn't the same as a bromide print. As such, they don't need to be constantly compared. They are both what they are.

In fact, you don't even need a digital camera to be able to digitally manipulate your work. Where digital printing can set you free is when you start considering the original photograph – whether it's digital or analogue – as just a starting point. You can do almost anything to and with this image with the help of imaging software. However, I feel obligated to pass on a warning at this stage.

As you become more competent with Photoshop® or other software, you can get to feel all-powerful and that you can make any old image look good – and that will make your photography sloppy.

■ **Whether you have** *a digital camera or a conventional film camera, you can use your computer, along with the relevant software, to manipulate your images.*

Nothing you can do on your computer will transform a bad picture into a good one. But if you shoot a great image, the computer can work wonders.

As a digital photographer, your ultimate aim is to be able to see in your mind's eye how you want the print to look *after* it's been through graphic manipulation. That way, you'll know what sort of original image you need in order to create the final image. If you don't know what you want the final image to be, how will you know what to shoot?

Which computer to choose?

IF YOU DON'T HAVE A COMPUTER, *or can't upgrade your present PC enough to accommodate your digital photography needs, you will have to buy one. That means you'll have to decide whether you want a PC or an Apple Mac™.*

There is no doubt that some 90 per cent of photographers, designers, artists, and publishers use Macs. It is generally accepted that Macs are easier to work with. On the newer models it's also easier to upgrade the amount of RAM on a Mac, which means you can increase your memory as you become more involved. Controlling colour is also easier on a Mac. (If you're a PC user, feel free to disagree, but these are my observations.) However, if you already own a PC and are pretty computer-literate, you'll manage just beautifully with the addition of Photoshop.

> **DEFINITION**
>
> RAM (said "ram", rather than as initials) stands for random access memory and is the memory-storage component of your computer. It is measured in **megabytes**, which you may also see or hear referred to as MB or megs.

Because photographic files are larger than text files, your main concern will be having enough RAM. To do anything serious you will need at least 64 **megabytes** free and available for use.

■ **Your choice of PC or Mac** *might be dictated by what your friends and relatives use. But do a bit of research; you may find that one system is better for the particular work you intend to do. If you travel a lot, for example, it may even be worth investing in a laptop computer.*

Peripherals

OF COURSE, AS WITH SO MUCH IN LIFE, *it doesn't end there. Having a computer is not enough: you need some other gear before you can get going.*

Graphics-manipulation packages

There is a handful of packages (also called applications or programs) available for your computer that you can use to manipulate your photographs. Perhaps the most well known of these is Adobe Photoshop. You can use these packages regardless of whether the pictures were shot on a conventional or digital camera. The only thing to remember is that before you can manipulate the image, the image must be digital.

 If you shot the picture on a digital camera, fine, you're laughing. You just need to connect your camera to your computer with the relevant lead (this probably came with the camera when you bought it) and follow the simple instructions in your camera's manual.

 If you shot the original image on a film camera, then you will have to digitize it first. You do this by scanning the picture. (If you don't know what a scanner is, don't worry – we'll be coming to that in a minute.)

Whichever route you have taken or will take, you will end up with a computer file, or electronic file, that contains your image.

Playing with the image

Once your image is an electronic file, you can import it into your manipulation program and the world is your oyster!

It's impossible for me to give you a tutorial on how to use your chosen application but I can give you a list of some of the sorts of effect you can achieve. The most basic manipulations you will need probably fall into one of the following categories:

 Compensation for over- or underexposure on the original shot; this can also be thought of as adjusting the overall brightness of the image

 Sharpness of the image

You can also consider making changes of the following types (among others), but you will then start to move away more dramatically from the look you originally wanted to capture:

 Contrast (that is, the degree of difference between the bright and dark areas of the original image)

 Colour saturation (the overall richness, or strength, of the colour in the picture)

Colour variation

On the subject of colour, be aware that the colours you see on your monitor will be different to the colours you'll get on your printout. You need to check out your computer manual and set up your monitor colours as closely as possible to the colours of your printer. Even then you will still need to experiment to get the best results.

Graphic tablets

If you start getting really involved with Photoshop and money becomes no object, a graphic tablet is a great tool to use instead of the mouse. It has a **_pressure-sensitive_** stylus that you use like a pen to draw on the tablet. It gives you easier control since you can draw around areas with great accuracy. A graphic tablet isn't essential, but if you are seriously into retouching and manipulation it'll make life much easier.

> **DEFINITION**
>
> The term **pressure sensitive** means pretty much what it says. But specifically, with items like graphic tablets, it means that you can create different effects by varying the pressure, just as you can with a pencil or paintbrush.

Printer　Speaker　Monitor　Hard drive

Graphic tablet　Keyboard　Mouse　Scanner

■ **Once you've got your computer** *you'll need some other bits too! Along with a graphics-manipulation package, a scanner, printer, and graphic tablet will be of great benefit to you.*

Scanners

Some computer deals include a basic scanner and printer, and these will be quite adequate to get you started. Most scanners are flatbed scanners, much like a photocopier. The scanner turns the print or document into digital language that can be used by your computer and printer to turn out digital prints. I would advise you to buy one with a transparency adapter so that you can scan transparencies or negatives.

Resolution for scans

How much resolution do you need when scanning a print or transparency? This is a much-debated point. The important questions to ask yourself are:

 What is the size of the original source image?

 What will the output size be? (This will probably be determined by how you want to use the image. For example, is it for your A4 home printer, or to be sent in an e-mail to a friend? Or are you going all the way to an A2 print that you want to exhibit?)

What will the output device be?

If you are producing a small postcard-size print or using the image on the Web, you only need a low-resolution scanner. There is no point in scanning at a higher resolution than you require because you will produce a larger file than you need, and that will be harder and slower to work with. An exhibition print, on the other hand, will require a higher resolution, which in turn will produce a larger file.

You will rarely need more than 25 MB for a photographic file.

■ **The capabilities** *of a scanner can vary greatly, depending largely on price. However, if you're concentrating mainly on small work, a cheap one can still produce some great results.*

Also the amount of PPIs you need depends on the size of the original images you are scanning. An APS neg requires more resolution to produce a good-quality A5 print than a 10 x 8-inch (25 x 20-cm) colour print will. But let's slip some common sense into this discussion. When brochures and magazines talk about high-quality prints, they are comparing digital prints to bromide prints. And if you are after bromide-quality digital prints, you are going to have to spend serious money on a top-of-the-range computer, scanner, and printer... and you still won't even get close.

> **DEFINITION**
>
> On screen, resolution is measured in **PPI** – pixels per inch. Printer resolution however, is measured in dots per inch, or **DPI**.

So forget all about that and you will find that you can produce really lovely-quality prints using basic scanners and printers. They will probably please you and that's what it's all about. So don't be intimidated by having too few PPIs and DPIs, just get on with the job at hand.

If you are doing lots of scanning of negatives or transparencies I would advise a self-contained film scanner that produces consistently high-quality results.

The hardware and software that you end up buying should reflect where you want to go with your images, creatively speaking. Don't buy stuff that you don't need or can't afford just to have as some sort of status symbol.

It's very important that you set up a sensible filing system for your images so that you can access them easily. I would suggest you name your files after how they look (for example, "boat by shore").

Printers

The standard printer – the sort of thing you'll get as part of your computer package, for example – is an ink-jet printer. These printers produce printouts by squirting (this isn't the technical term!) dots of colour and tone. The resolution is therefore measured by how many DPIs the printer can reproduce. The latest printers are very good value for money. Even an inexpensive one can produce surprisingly good prints. However, to create a huge poster of one of your favourite images, use a professional printing house.

It's important to point out that, as with traditional photography, it's not the equipment that takes photographs – it ultimately comes down to the talent of the photographer using the equipment. Digital imaging is the same. Sure, the resolution and equipment are important, but more important is your ability and your personal creative input. The more effort you put into getting to know your equipment and the more you experiment with it, the better your digital photography will become.

The paper you use in your printer is very important to the quality of your end print, and there is an enormous variety of surfaces available now. If you want the ultimate in definition, use a glossy photographic-style paper. If, on the other hand, you want a soft, romantic feel to the print, you could use an uncoated watercolour paper.

It's vital to check out the deals being offered by your computer stockists. It's very competitive out there and there are some great bargains to be had, so be pushy and get what you want.

■ **As with scanners,** *you get what you pay for with a printer. But, these days, the technology is so good that even a relatively small sum of money can get you some pretty impressive results.*

You may be able to get a program like Adobe Photoshop with your printer as part of the deal. Most likely it will be a pared-down version of the latest one available, but it can serve you very well at little or no extra cost.

CD writer

It's essential that you make back-up copies of your photographic files. The best way to do this is by *writing*, or *burning*, them on to a CD. This makes more sense than putting them on to any other back-up medium because CDs have a greater storage capacity and are much cheaper to buy.

A CD writer is also an essential purchase if you are going to be sending work to clients or potential clients.

■ **The best way to back up:**
Your computer may come with a CD writer built in, but if it doesn't you should buy one, because it's an essential item.

Case study: Graeme Harris

MY FRIEND AND PHOTOGRAPHIC COLLEAGUE *Graeme Harris is a distinguished photographer and printmaker who has recently been printing on his computer instead of in the darkroom. He still prints traditionally, too, but is experimenting with his computer to produce a different look or style to his work.*

I twisted Graeme's arm to let you see the step-by-step process behind one of his new images. Here's what he had to say.

 This original picture of whitebait fish was shot on HP5+ film using a 55mm macro lens on a 35mm camera. I lit the fish with window light and put a white reflector opposite the window. This has produced the highlight along the bellies of the fish. To give a suggestion of a golden-brownish colour I slightly sepia-toned the print. This has created enough colour to warrant me scanning it in colour. I could, of course, have opted to scan it as a straight black-and-white print and then colour it in Photoshop later.

The original print measured 12.63 x 19.3 cm (5 x 7½ inches). I scanned it on a flatbed scanner, creating a 5.6 MB file, then adjusted the brightness and contrast of the image. This is really something that can only be done to suit your own personal taste.

THE ORIGINAL WHITEBAIT PICTURE

2 The next thing I did was crop the top and bottom of the image slightly – once again to personal taste. Resized in Photoshop, the picture size is now 15.82 x 12.63 cm (6¼ x 5 inches), and the file size is 4.61 MB.

3 Using Photoshop, I lightened up each eye, adding a highlight to make the eyes (and the fish) look more alive. I also removed some dust spots. I played around with the colour curves to dramatically change the colour. I wanted to produce a more abstract image than the original, something looking like a silkscreen print.

CROPPED AND RESIZED

This process can take many or few steps, depending on what sort of effect you are trying to achieve. I adjusted each of the primary red, blue, green colours separately. First was blue (input 43, output 164), then green (input 145, output 255), and finally red (input 107, output 8).

The number of possible combinations – and overall potential – is really quite overwhelming, and once you start adding the overlay and filter possibilities it can all get a bit mind-blowing. The bottom line is personal taste. What I might find to be a charming image, you may not, and vice versa. You have to create work that, first and foremost, will be pleasing to you.

THE FINISHED ARTWORK

If you are just getting started, don't be put off by curves and inputs and outputs. It makes more sense once you get going.

Case study: Maud Larsson

MAUD LARSSON is a young freelance photographer who has been my
brave assistant on this book. She has worked as a traditional printer (in both
colour and black-and-white) for a number of years. But she is definitely part
of the new generation, and she has moved her work further into digital
printmaking in order to increase the creative scope of her pictures, which, at
the moment, are made mostly for the creatively demanding music industry.

Maud has contributed some of her images and I thought it best to let her describe her
approach in her own words.

Not better, just different

Photoshop is a terrific imaging software package. It does all your usual darkroom work
and more. For me the benefit of digital printmaking is that it takes you
further, and without chemicals. It's more flexible, mobile, and easier to use.

*I've never understood why people compare the quality or outcome of
digital with analogue photographic printmaking. They are both forms
of expression, which is why arguing that one is "more real" or "worth
more" just seems a waste of energy to me.*

What we today call "alternative processes", like all the old-school and not-so-
straightforward ways of working (cyanotype, lith printing, salt printing, Van Dyke
prints, and bromoil printing, for example), never had to fight any battles with whatever
processes preceded them.

Printmaking in the darkroom is still something else entirely. Here the magic is of a more
physical kind. If you're after a traditional-looking photographic image, use your
traditional darkroom. If you're interested in old, alternative printmaking, where you
print images using sunlight or liquid photographic emulsion, then do it. But if you want
a new and interesting way of working with imagery, there's Photoshop.

Of course there are important issues to be aware of with regards to retouching,
manipulation, and digital enhancement. Then there's your responsibility as a
photographer, too. But photographs were always a construction of one person's reality
(whatever that reality is) seen through a camera. Add to that the choice of printing
method, context, and the viewer's response....

There's far more to be gained by avoiding labels like "traditional quality" and "real photography" than there is by adhering to them.

Generally I like to just twist and turn the imagery I've got to work with. I like to see where it takes me. The original medium may be photographic, artwork, scanned media, or various combinations of all these (this brings copyright into focus!). Then... well, it turns into something else – something that reflects how I feel. Usually it comes out looking like a fine-art relation.

I don't always know what effect a particular filter is going to have on an image. It's never a case of "I'll apply this because then X will follow"; more like, "Maybe this will take me somewhere interesting". When I start off, I may have a vague idea of where I want the image to go, but that can change completely while I'm working, usually due to happy accidents.

Photoshop is truly fantastic – an advanced and creative toy. Go play!

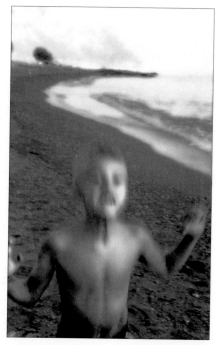

■ **Yannis Viglis:** *This image originated from a transparency that I printed on to negative paper (C-type paper), but it was put through a transparency process – that is, it was turned into a negative image and then back into a positive one. This shouldn't really be taken to extremes since it messes up the chemistry. I've used it here simply for the sheer intensity of effect. It turned the print into a blue-toned image. I scanned the picture, sharpened my dear cousin Yannis, and used the "diffuse glow" filter. Then I faded it until I was happy with the look.*

■ **The Sad Man:** *I wanted to illustrate what sadness can do to someone, or what someone can turn sadness into. Many people, for their own reasons, feel more comfortable being unhappy than not. This picture was originally a straight, but very dark, photograph, looking nothing like this final print. I lightened it, stretched the whole of the guy's body, and made his eyes larger.*

■ **Benjamin Waiting for the Bus:** *This was originally a black-and-white photograph. I worked with Photoshop's "pinch" and "glass" filters, together with various levels of fading of both.*

■ **The Latecomers:** *This is Brian Quinn, songwriter and main vocalist of The Latecomers. To increase the amount of blue in this picture, I used curves and the channel mixer, fading where appropriate.*

INTERNET

www.atsf.co.uk/ilight/
tech/colmap2.html

This web page shows some of the effects you can create by playing around with the colour channels in Adobe Photoshop.

■ **Maja in Winter:** *Crete, right at the turn of the 21st century. This was originally a black-and-white photograph of Maja, my younger sister. I used Photoshop's "diffuse glow" filter, and I worked a lot with curves and fading back and forth.*

A simple summary

✔ The computer is simply another means of expanding your levels of creativity. It's not intended to replace the old methods – it just offers an alternative.

✔ The two types of computer to choose from are PCs and Macs.

✔ You need some other hardware and software if you want to manipulate your pictures.

✔ A graphics-manipulation package like Photoshop is an essential purchase. The effects you can achieve are almost limitless.

✔ If you intend to work with shots taken with a traditional (rather than digital) camera, you will need to scan them first.

✔ A printer is vital if you want a physical version of your finished image.

✔ Burning your work on to CD is the best way to back it up. Blank CDs are now very cheap to buy.

Photography on the Web

THERE IS A HUGE AMOUNT *of information about photography on the Internet. The following list contains some of the sites that I think are most useful. Please note, though, that due to the fast-changing nature of the Net, some of these sites may be out of date by the time you read this. Happy hunting!*

www.a1.nl/phomepag/markerink/af_expla.htm
This link takes you to an explanation of how autofocus works.

www.acp.au.com/
This is the web site of the Australian Centre for Photography – a not-for-profit organization established in 1973 and located in Paddington, Sydney.

www.amateurphoto.about.com/hobbies/amateurphoto /library/bllenses.htm?terms=lenses
This page has some good information on lenses as well as some tips on filters.

www.amateurphoto.about.com/hobbies/amateurphoto /library/weekly/aa030498.htm
Check out this web page for some great still-life tips.

www.amphot.co.uk/content/creatmono/cm2.htm
You can subscribe to *Photo Art International* and *Digital Photo Art* magazines at this web site.

www.aophoto.co.uk
This is the web site of The Association of Photographers. Among other things, it contains a huge selection of work by its members that may inspire your own creativity.

www.apogeephoto.com/apr2001/ratty042001.shtml
This page of Apogee Photo's web site is entitled "Seven Steps For Better Point-and-Shoot Pictures" and offers you just what it says.

www.apogeephoto.com/buyguide/index1.htm
Click on "Film" in the category list for a selection of film manufacturers. There's a detailed product guide for each company.

www.apogeephoto.com/PFYP.shtml
This web page is called "Photography for Young People", but it's great for beginners of all ages. The topics covered change from time to time, so take a look.

www.artisdead.net
This site contains not just photography, but a range of work from several fields of the arts. There are often some very interesting photographs here, though, so check it out!

www.artzone.gr
The Black-and-White ArtZone web site is dedicated to black-and-white photography.

www.atsf.co.uk/ilight/tech/colmap2.html
This web page shows some of the effects you can create by playing around with the colour channels in Adobe Photoshop®.

www.azuswebworks.com/photography/
Go to this web site and click on "Camera Basics" in the left-hand column. Scroll down for a look at how the camera's aperture and shutter work.

www.betterphoto.com/exploring/groenhoutExposure.asp
This web page is well worth visiting: it contains an interesting article called "Obtaining Correct Exposure".

www.camerareview.com
This is a great place to start if you're not sure which SLR camera to buy. You can even type in which features you're looking for, and the site will come back with a list of cameras that fit the bill.

www.corbijn.co.uk
This is the official Anton Corbijn web site. It contains a good selection of his work, with each picture annotated by Corbijn himself.

www.dpict.org
DPICT (incorporating *Creative Camera*) is "the new magazine of camera culture" and this is its home page. See what's in the latest magazine, subscribe, or buy back issues.

www.dpreview.com
Unbiased, in-depth reviews of most of the current digital camera models can be found at this great web site.

www.explorephotography.com/
This site has tips on photography techniques and buying cameras and lenses, as well as depth-of-field charts and articles on all manner of photographic topics.

www.fodors.com/focus
This web page, "How to Take Travel Pictures Like a Pro", gives some great hints and tips for the travel photographer.

www.friendsofphotography.org
This is the web site of The Friends of Photography – a non-profit, international visual-arts organization that operates the Ansel Adams Center for Photography in San Francisco.

www.geocities.com/clickbrah/surfphototips.htm
Check out this web page for tips on how to photograph surfing action.

www.geocities.com/cokinfiltersystem
This is an unbiased, independent analysis of Cokin filters, the world's leading range of special-effects filters.

goaustralia.about.com/library/weekly/blimages.htm?terms=australian+photography
This site contains a whole load of great pictures from all over Australia.

www.howstuffworks.com/digital-camera2htm
This in-depth look at how digital cameras work is recommended reading.

www.libraryofphotography.com/
This is a great resource for photographers, packed with information, links to other sites, and great pictures.

www.masters-of-photography.com/
This site boasts a selection of works by some of the greats, including Ansel Adams, Alfred Stieglitz, and Edward Weston.

members.home.net/gillettm/DOF.html
> This web page contains a depth-of-field calculator, which you can use "to find the near, far, and hyperfocal distance for a specific lens".

www.midland-7.org/moutray/photography.htm
> Entitled "Photography: The Basics", this web page contains a history of photography, how to make a pinhole camera, black-and-white printing, and loads of other stuff.

www.nyip.com/tips/topic_art0700.html
> This web page contains the New York Institute of Photography's "Tips for Better Photographs".

www.photodirect.com.au
> This is a great web site promoting Australian photographs and photography.

www.photography.about.com/arts/photography/library/weekly/aa071999.htm
> "Who's Ansel Adams?", you ask! This is as good a place as any to find out.

www.photography.about.com/arts/photography/library/weekly/aa122099.htm?terms=Home+Lighting
> This is a useful article on how to photograph celebrations, parties, and other events that take place indoors.

www.photographybygarrett.com
> This is my own web site. Why not visit and see if there's anything you like?

www.photography.ca/otherartists/karsh.html
> This web page has a handful of portraits by Yousuf Karsh as well as a brief biography of this important portraitist.

www.photogs.com/bwworld
> The Black-and-White World web site describes itself as "a celebration of photography" and is packed with great articles, pictures, and tips.

www.photo.net
> Photography tips, equipment reviews, learning forums, photographers' portfolios, and chat rooms can all be found here.

www.photosecrets.com/tips.htm
> *PhotoSecrets* is a series of travel guides aimed at photographers. This web page contains a whole load of useful tips.

www.phototechmag.com/previous-articles/2000/capinegro-mar/cappi1.htm
> This sample article from *PHOTO Techniques* magazine is called "Re-orchestrating Light" and is in the series "The Art of Photoshop".

www.phototechmag.com/previous-articles/2000/lane-july/lane1.htm
> This is a great article on photographing children. The author has built up a stock photography business with her pictures.

www.phototechmag.com/previous-articles/sept99-kerr/kerr1.htm
> This article, "Controlling Light for Photography", offers a great analysis of what can be achieved with just one studio light.

www.phototechmag.com/previous-articles/sept99-mort.htm
> This great article, on *PHOTO Techniques* magazine's web site, sings the praises of 6 x 6-cm medium format photography.

www.photoweb.ndirect.co.uk
Photoweb UK claims to be Britain's number-one site for photographers. In its 80 pages are 300 pictures and over 300 links to other sites.

www.pinholevisions.org/
Pinhole Visions is a great resource for those who are interested in pinhole photography. There is a fantastic gallery of pictures by a number of artists.

www.psa-photo.org/gallery.htm
This is the gallery page of the Photographic Society of America.

www.rleggat.com/photohistory
This is a great web site for information about some of photography's pioneers. Not only is there a history of the art form up until the 1920s, but all the key names are cross-referenced: just click on a name in the text to jump to the relevant biography.

www.rps.org
This is the web site of England's Royal Photographic Society, which was formed 150 years ago with Queen Victoria and Prince Albert as patrons.

www.snappysnaps.com
This is the web site of Snappy Snaps, *Amateur Photographer* magazine's "High Street Lab of the Year" for 5 successive years.

www.teleport.com/~pacrim/storys/milan/95-02x.htm
This is an interesting glossary of sorts: it contains words and phrases that you might hear from second-hand camera dealers… and what they really mean!

www.thirdeyephoto.com
The great Third Eye Photowork Collection web site exhibits many photographs taken from unusual points of view.

ubmail.ubalt.edu/~dhaynes/photo/depth.htm
This web page contains an article on depth of field from *Introduction to Photography* by David Barnes.

www.view.com.au/dombrovskis/index.html
This link takes you to information about and pictures by the late photographer Peter Dombrovskis, whose work is on show in places as esteemed as the National Gallery of Victoria, Australia.

www.west-crete.com/photos.htm
This is something of a curio – a web site that only contains landscape photographs of the Greek island of Crete.

www.wises.com.au/
The Wise's Wilderness web site (named after its creator, photographer Geoff Wise) contains some beautiful photographs of the Australia that few people get to see, as well as photography hints and tips.

www2.southwind.net/~tkalp/pw2/Comp.htm
This page of Wichita South High School's web site contains some sound advice on photographic composition.

Further reading

THERE ARE SO MANY photography books and magazines on the market these days that it's almost impossible to select what to recommend. The choices that I have made here reflect my own personal interests to a great extent, but I really think that you should read as much as you can and look at as many photographers' pictures as possible.

Books

Ansel Adams
Any book by or about Ansel Adams is worth reading.

Tom Ang
Digital Photography (Mitchell Beazley)

Diane Arbus
An Aperture Monograph (Aperture)

Marc Atkins and Iain Sinclair
Liquid City (Reaktion Books)

Richard Avedon
Evidence (Eastman-Kodak)

John Berger and Jean Mohr
Another Way of Telling (Vintage Books)

Henri Cartier Bresson
The World of Cartier Bresson (Thames and Hudson)

Graham Clarke
The Photograph (Oxford Books)

Anton Corbijn
Famouz (Schirmer Mosel)
Star Trak (Schirmer Mosel)

Edward S. Curtis and Hans Christian Adams
Edward S. Curtis (Taschen)

Eddie Ephramus
What's Missing? Realising Our Photographic Potential (Argentum)

Elliott Erwitt
Photographs Antiphotographs (New York Graphic Society)

Max Ferguson
Max Ferguson's Digital Darkroom Masterclass (Focal Press)

John Garrett
John Garrett's Black-and-White Photography Masterclass (Collins & Brown)

Ralph Gibson
L'Histoire of France (Aperture)

Ernst Haas
In America (Thames and Hudson)

Andre Kertesz
60 Years of Photography (Thames and Hudson)

Ralph Eugene Meatyard
An American Visionary
(Akron Art Museum)
An Aperture Monograph
(Aperture)

Duane Michals
Duane Duck
(Museum of Modern Art Oxford)

Irving Penn
Passage (Stropf/Callaway)

W. Eugene Smith
The Camera as Conscience
(Thames and Hudson)

Chris Wainwright
The Creative Darkroom Handbook (Cassell)

Randall Webb and Martin Reed
Spirits of Salts (Argentum)

Donovan Wylie
Losing Ground (Fourth Estate)

Magazines

Amateur Photographer
This British magazine was launched over 115 years ago and claims to be "the world's number-one photo weekly magazine".

American Photo
Published six times a year and aimed at professionals and advanced or aspiring photographers. Includes articles on equipment, technique, and industry developments.

Aperture
This slightly pricey quarterly photography magazine has been described by leading professionals as "the most serious and the most valuable periodical in the photographic world". Need I say more?

Outdoor Photographer
Written by the world's leading landscape, wildlife, sports, and travel photographers. Published ten times a year.

PC Photo
Dedicated to computers and photography. Includes advice on effects, as well as reviews and tips.

PHOTOgraphic
Monthly magazine for all camera enthusiasts. Packed with tips, techniques, and product reviews.

Popular Photography
This monthly is aimed at beginners as well as professionals. Every issue is packed with tips to help you improve your photographic prowess.

A simple glossary

Aperture The adjustable diameter of a lens, the size of which determines how much light is able to reach the film. Aperture size is measured in f-numbers, or f-stops. *See also* f-number.

Aperture priority A mode on a semi-automatic camera, whereby you select the setting for the aperture and the camera automatically sets the correct shutter speed to make the exposure.

APS Stands for Advanced Photo System, a type of camera launched in the mid-1990s.

ASA Stands for American Standards Association and was the measurement of film speed before ISO was adopted. *See also* ISO.

Available light This is a term used to describe photography utilizing existing light only. Often available-light photography refers to pictures taken in low light. Many of the most moving and powerful reportage photographs ever taken have been available-light pictures. Unfortunately, too many photographers seem to have lost the art of this type of photography and allowed the flash to take over. With the fast film available today there is virtually no situation that cannot be photographed without flash.

Back-light Light that comes from behind the subject in a photograph. Can sometimes cause problems with exposures leading to the need for a back-light compensation (BLC) function. *See also* Back-light compensation.

Back-light compensation A function available on many cameras these days, for use when the light from behind a subject is so bright that the subject would be underexposed.

Between-the-lens shutter *See* Leaf shutter.

Blow-up A term used to mean a large print.

Bracket To bracket exposures means to take a series of exposures both under and over the meter reading. With your SLR you will most probably have an exposure-compensation facility that allows you to go up to +2 stops and down to -2 stops in ⅓-of-a-stop increments.

Camera obscura This is a Latin term and literally means dark room, or dark chamber. It is also an early form of the camera as we know it today.

Chromogenic Means "as colour", *chrom(os)* being Greek for colour. These films are black-and-white but can be processed and printed as colour film.

Clip test A test in which a short piece of film – about three frames – is cut off the start of the film and developed to test whether your exposures are perfect.

Colour cast An unnatural colour that affects a print. Often these are true reflections of the scene at the time of shooting, but the human eye and brain had compensated for the colour discrepancy. The camera cannot do the same.

Colour-correction filter A filter that is used to either add a little warmth to or cool down the overall feel of a scene.

Colour negative Colour negative film produces a negative, or reverse, image, from which your print is made. You will hear people refer to colour negative film as print film.

Colour temperature The colour of light, or colour temperature, is calculated in degrees Kelvin (° K). For example, midday is between 5200 and 5400° K. Colour temperature readings are taken on a colour temperature meter, and from this reading you can work out what you need in terms of filters or camera/lens settings to get your desired colour effect.

Compact camera The correct term for a point-and-shoot camera. Usually a small, automatic 35mm camera with a direct-vision viewfinder.

Dedicated flash This is a flashgun designed by camera manufacturers to work only with their own make of cameras.

Depth of focus The distance in front and behind your picture's point of focus that is kept sharp. It is also known as depth of field.

Development Converting of an exposed film's latent image into a visible image. *See also* Latent image.

Diffuser A material that is used to soften or spread the light from a light source.

Direct-vision viewfinder A viewfinder that allows the photographer a direct look at the scene, which is not exactly what the lens "sees".

Downrating *See* Pulling.

DPI Printer resolution is measured in dots per inch, or DPI.

80B filter This is a blue filter that restores the colour temperature of tungsten light back to daylight.

Exposure The amount of light permitted on to the film. Also the length of time the light is allowed to act on the film.

Exposure latitude The amount a film can be under- or overexposed and still produce a satisfactory print.

Film speed A film's sensitivity to light, measured in ISO numbers. The higher the number, the faster the film, and the greater its sensitivity to light.

Filter A glass, plastic, or gelatine disk that is placed over a lens to alter the appearance of the scene being photographed.

Fixed-focal-length lens A lens that does not have zoom capabilities.

Flash throw Used to mean the distance from the camera that the flash will light adequately for a photograph.

f-number The measurement of a lens's aperture. The f-number is a fraction of the focal length of the lens, so f2 on a 50mm lens would mean that the aperture is 25 mm. f-numbers are also called f-stops.

Focal-plane shutter Almost universal in SLR cameras, the focal-plane shutter is basically a curtain with a slit that travels across the film plane exposing the film. Some designs use two curtains. The focal-plane shutter is positioned at the back of the camera, in front of the film.

Focal point The point in a picture to which you wish to bring the viewer's attention.

Frame Used to describe the area of the world that you see through your camera's viewfinder.

f-stop *See* f-number.

Hard neg This is the term given to a high-contrast negative. A low-contrast neg is called a soft neg.

Iris diaphragm Adjustable mechanism of metal blades that forms the aperture. Also called a diaphragm.

ISO Abbreviation for International Standards Organization and the unit of measurement of a film's sensitivity to light. Some of your old cameras and books will have an ASA rating. They are exactly the same as ISO ratings. *See also* Film speed.

Kelvin Unit of measurement used to describe the colour temperature of light, degrees Kelvin (° K).

Kodak® The trademark Kodak is a word George Eastman made up – he just liked the sound of it – he also thought the visual appearance of it would look good and be remembered. It doesn't mean anything!

Latent image The invisible image made by the chemical reaction of light on the film's emulsion.

LCD Stands for liquid crystal display.

Leaf shutter A shutter system built into a lens rather than into a camera body (as is the case with the focal-plane shutter), so called because of the series of overlapping leaves that allow it to expose the film.

Megabytes The unit of measurement for the memory of a computer. You may also see or hear them referred to as MB or megs.

Megapixel One million pixels. Also known as MP.

Noise Digital jargon meaning a break-up of the image; similar to grain on film or interference on your TV.

Opening up Term used to mean increasing the size of the aperture in order to allow more light to expose the film.

Overexpose To allow too much light to reach the film.

Pan The word pan is a verb meaning to move the camera in the same direction as a moving subject, always keeping the subject in approximately the same position within the frame. Panning is also used in TV and the movies to follow the on-screen action, and in music meaning to move sound from one speaker to another.

Pinhole camera A light-tight box with a pinhole instead of a lens through which light is transmitted to a piece of film directly opposite.

Pixel The easiest way to define a pixel is to think of it as one tile of a Roman wall mosaic. Each tile has only one colour, but when all the tiles are creatively arranged, you have a complete picture.

Point-and-shoot This is the name often given to compact cameras, simply because it more or less defines the actions needed to take a photograph with those machines. The trade and professional photographers tend to use the term compact camera instead.

PPI On a computer screen resolution is measured in PPI – pixels per inch.

Pulling This term means to expose a film to more light than its ISO rating dictates. Also called downrating.

Pushing This term means to expose a film to less light than its ISO rating dictates. You need to tell your lab if you do this because they will need to develop the film differently. Pushing is sometimes also known as uprating.

Pressure sensitive Means pretty much what it says. But specifically, with items like graphic tablets, it means that you can create different effects by varying the pressure, just as you can with a pencil or paintbrush.

Quality Photographers use this word as an all-embracing term that covers sharpness, grain size, colour saturation, and contrast.

RAM (said "ram", rather than as initials) Stands for random access memory and is the memory-storage component of your computer.

RC paper The RC stands for resin-coated. Most printmakers still use a paper-based material called fibre-based, or FB, paper.

Reflector Any material that reflects, or bounces, light. Reflectors are usually white or off-white to reduce the possibility of colour casts.

Selective focus When you focus on one plane and throw the rest out of focus by using a large aperture this is known as selective focus.

Shutter The mechanism that you use to control when and for how long the film inside the camera is exposed to light. It is activated by pressing the button that "takes the picture". The button is correctly called the shutter button or shutter-release button.

Shutter priority A mode on a semi-automatic camera, whereby you select the shutter speed and the camera automatically sets the correct aperture to make the exposure.

SLR Stands for single lens reflex and is a camera design in which, through the use of an angled mirror and a series of silver surfaces, the scene in the viewfinder is exactly the same as that "seen" by the lens.

Soft focus Means out of focus, giving a soft edge to the subjects.

Soft neg The term given to a low-contrast negative. A high-contrast neg is called a hard neg.

Stopping down Term meaning to close down the aperture, minimizing the amount of light allowed to expose the film.

Surrealists The Surrealists created paintings, drawings, and photographs that were inspired by dreams. Salvador Dalí, Pablo Picasso, and Marcel Duchamp were the leaders of the movement. Man Ray was the most famous Surrealist photographer.

Telephoto lens A compact, long-focal-length lens. Also called a tele lens.

Tonal management This term describes a photographer's ability to compose a picture that consists of a pleasing arrangement of tones.

Transparency The professional term for a slide.

TTL metering Through-the-lens light metering.

Uprating See Pushing.

Viewfinder A system through which the photographer is able to see what he or she is shooting.

Writing The act of making copies of your work on to a CD is known as writing, or burning. It's not as scary as it sounds – in fact it's not that dissimilar to copying on to floppy disks in the old days!

Index

Acknowledgments

AUTHOR'S ACKNOWLEDGMENTS

I owe many thanks to the following people:

Michelle Garrett for supplying many of her images for this book and also for helping me with picture editing; Graeme Harris for sound advice and for supplying illustrations and copy on the Digital Darkroom chapter; Maud Larsson for all her patient work as my assistant on this project and for her prints and copy on the Digital Darkroom chapter; Mary Thompson at DK for commissioning this book and for general support; designer Simon Murrell and editor David Tombesi-Walton for their skill and humour throughout the process. A final thanks is due to my sons Nick and Matt who are the subjects of many of the pictures, plus all the brave souls who wittingly or unwittingly contributed to this book.

PACKAGER'S ACKNOWLEDGMENTS

Sands Publishing Solutions would like to thank the following people for their help in this project: Hilary Bird for compiling the index; Jessops of Maidstone for the loan of equipment for photography purposes; Barry Robson for the dog illustrations; Hayley Smith at Dorling Kindersley's picture library; Mariana Sonnenberg at ilumi for picture research; Frank Spence for the loan of his digital camera. A special thanks also to John Garrett for making this project such a pleasure.

PICTURE CREDITS

Apple Computer UK Ltd: 325.
Canon: 54, 58 br, 77, 80 cr, 82 cr, 85 bl, 315 ct.
Corbis UK: 96.
Dorling Kindersley: 20; Science Museum, London 24; Musée Gauguin, Tahiti 26; 27, 29, 30, 38, 146, 263, 267, 269, 286, 291, 327; Philip Gatward 55, 58; Steve Gorton 42, 218 cr; Dave King 314 tr; Stephen Oliver 218 br, 289. All © Dorling Kindersley. For further information see: www.dkimages.com
Fuji: 32, 80 br, 83, 84, 85 tr, 86, 282, 315, 324 bl.
Gandolfi Ltd: 290.
Michelle Garrett: 67, 78, 125, 140, 144, 159 bl & br, 168, 170, 174, 179 b, 180 b, 220, 223, 225, 227, 228–9, 230, 231, 281.

Graeme Harris: 74, 284, 331, 332.
Hasselblad: 287.
Hewlett Packard: 330 tr.
Hulton Getty: 22, 25, 28.
Iomega: 318, 330 br.
Maud Larsson: 322, 334, 335, 336, 337.
Janos Marffy: 31.
Simon Murrell: 36, 37, 43, 44 tr, 48, 56, 62, 64, 65, 71, 90, 93, 94, 306, 316.
Nikon: 33, 81, 324 br.
Sony: 317.
UMAX Systems: 328.

All other images © John Garrett.

Key:
t=top; b=bottom; l=left;
r=right; c=centre